Biography Today

Profiles of People of Interest to Young Readers

Volume 16
Issue 2
April 2007

Cherie D. Abbey
Managing Editor

*615 Griswold Street
Detroit, Michigan 48226*

Cherie D. Abbey, *Managing Editor*
Kevin Hillstrom, *Editor*

Allison A. Beckett, Laurie DiMauro, Sheila Fitzgerald, Joan Goldsworthy, Jeff Hill, Anne J. Johnson, Justin Karr, Leslie Karr, Eve Nagler, Diane Telgen, *Sketch Writers*

Allison A. Beckett, Mary Butler, and Linda Strand, *Research Staff*

* * *

Peter E. Ruffner, *Publisher*
Frederick G. Ruffner, Jr., *Chairman*
Matthew P. Barbour, *Senior Vice President*
Kay Gill, *Vice President — Directories*

* * *

David P. Bianco, *Marketing Director*
Elizabeth Collins, *Research and Permissions Coordinator*
Kevin Hayes, *Operations Manager*
Barry Puckett, *Librarian*
Cherry Stockdale, *Permissions Assistant*

Shirley Amore, Martha Johns, Kirk Kauffman, and Johnny Lawrence, *Administrative Staff*

ISSN 1058-2347 • ISBN-13 978-0-7808-0970-3

This book is printed on acid-free paper meeting the ANSI Z39.48 Standard. The infinity symbol that appears above indicates that the paper in this book meets that standard.

Printed in the United States

Contents

Preface

Biography Today is a magazine designed and written for the young reader—ages 9 and above—and covers individuals that librarians and teachers tell us that young people want to know about most: entertainers, athletes, writers, illustrators, cartoonists, and political leaders.

The Plan of the Work

The publication was especially created to appeal to young readers in a format they can enjoy reading and readily understand. Each issue contains approximately 10 sketches arranged alphabetically. Each entry provides at least one picture of the individual profiled, and bold-faced rubrics lead the reader to information on birth, youth, early memories, education, first jobs, marriage and family, career highlights, memorable experiences, hobbies, and honors and awards. Each of the entries ends with a list of easily accessible sources designed to lead the student to further reading on the individual and a current address. Retrospective entries are also included, written to provide a perspective on the individual's entire career.

Biographies are prepared by Omnigraphics editors after extensive research, utilizing the most current materials available. Those sources that are generally available to students appear in the list of further reading at the end of the sketch.

Indexes

Cumulative indexes are an important component of *Biography Today*. Each issue of the *Biography Today* General Series includes a Cumulative Names Index, which comprises all individuals profiled in *Biography Today* since the series began in 1992. In addition, we compile three other indexes: the Cumulative General Index, Places of Birth Index, and Birthday Index. See our web site, www.biographytoday.com, for these three indexes, along with the Names Index. All *Biography Today* indexes are cumulative, including all individuals profiled in both the General Series and the Subject Series.

Our Advisors

This series was reviewed by an Advisory Board comprised of librarians, children's literature specialists, and reading instructors to ensure that the concept of this publication — to provide a readable and accessible biographical magazine for young readers — was on target. They evaluated the title as it developed, and their suggestions have proved invaluable. Any errors, however, are ours alone. We'd like to list the Advisory Board members, and to thank them for their efforts.

Gail Beaver
Adjunct Lecturer
University of Michigan
Ann Arbor, MI

Cindy Cares
Youth Services Librarian
Southfield Public Library
Southfield, MI

Carol A. Doll
School of Information Science and Policy
University of Albany, SUNY
Albany, NY

Kathleen Hayes-Parvin
Language Arts Teacher
Birney Middle School
Southfield, MI

Karen Imarisio
Assistant Head of Adult Services
Bloomfield Twp. Public Library
Bloomfield Hills, MI

Rosemary Orlando
Director
St. Clair Shores Public Library
St. Clair Shores, MI

Our Advisory Board stressed to us that we should not shy away from controversial or unconventional people in our profiles, and we have tried to follow their advice. The Advisory Board also mentioned that the sketches might be useful in reluctant reader and adult literacy programs, and we would value any comments librarians might have about the suitability of our magazine for those purposes.

Your Comments Are Welcome

Our goal is to be accurate and up-to-date, to give young readers information they can learn from and enjoy. Now we want to know what you think. Take a look at this issue of *Biography Today,* on approval. Write or call me with your comments. We want to provide an excellent source of biographical information for young people. Let us know how you think we're doing.

Cherie Abbey
Managing Editor, *Biography Today*
Omnigraphics, Inc.
615 Griswold Street
Detroit, MI 48226

editor@biographytoday.com
www.biographytoday.com

Congratulations!

Congratulations to the following individuals and libraries, who are receiving a free copy of *Biography Today*, Vol. 16, No. 2, for suggesting people who appear in this issue:

Fox Hills Elementary School Library, Indianapolis, IN

M. Deheck Fuqua, Naples, Italy

Sarah Jow, Reedley, CA

F. G. Ruffner, Jr., Grosse Pointe, MI

St. George Parish School/Fifth Grade, Seattle, WA

S.A. Schene, Homecroft Elementary School, Indianapolis, IN

Tzouanakis Intermediate, Greencastle, IN

Vassar High School Library, Vassar, MI

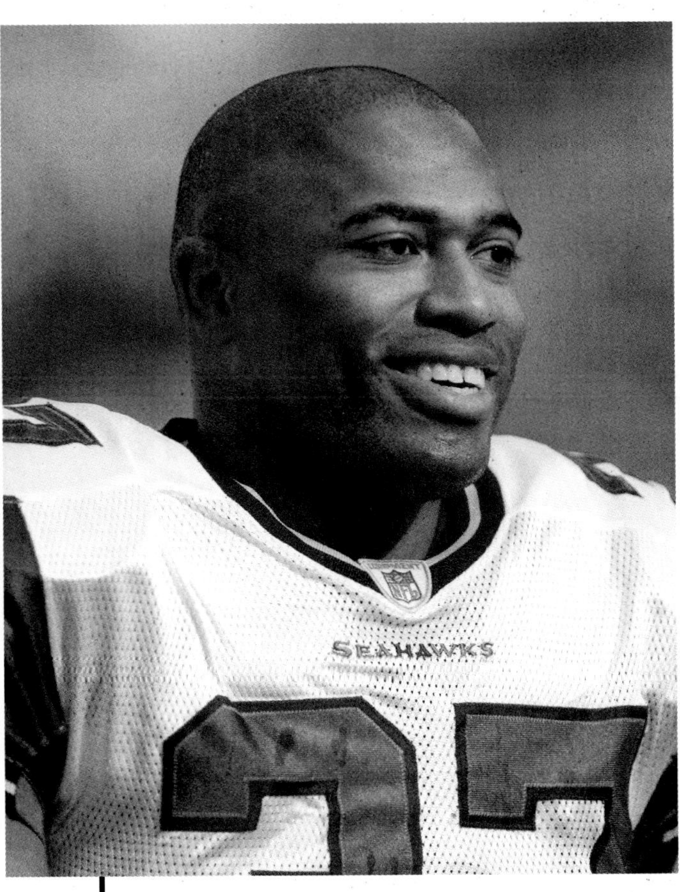

Shaun Alexander 1977-

American Professional Football Player with the Seattle Seahawks
NFL Most Valuable Player in 2005

BIRTH

Shaun Alexander was born on August 30, 1977, in Florence, Kentucky. His father, Curtis Alexander Jr., lives in Cincinnati, Ohio, which is situated a few miles from Florence on the north side of the Ohio River. He is employed by the chemical division of the salt producer Morton International. Carol Alexander, his mother, works in the truancy department of the Boone County School District in northern Kentucky.

Durran Alexander, Shaun's older brother by one year, serves as the executive director of the Shaun Alexander Foundation. Alexander also has three older half-brothers and four older half-sisters from his father's previous marriage; all of his half-siblings were raised by their mother in Cincinnati.

YOUTH

Alexander grew up in Boone County, Kentucky, a few miles south of Cincinnati. Although his home town of Florence at one time abounded with tobacco and dairy farms, it is now the second largest city in northern Kentucky and home to both a thoroughbred horse race track and a minor-league baseball stadium.

"[My mother] was the queen of discipline. She kept things very strict in our home," Alexander recalled. "But Mom balanced her discipline with love." His mother also taught him the importance of integrity of character and self-discipline. "I am who I am because I had a wise mother, who not only took me to church . . . but has lived the life she taught me to live."

Alexander's parents divorced when he was 11 years old. Consequently, he and his brother Durran were raised by their mother in a two-bedroom apartment in a government housing complex. "We had that main room, that little room, and that was everything," he explained. Despite his modest upbringing, however, Alexander never considered himself underprivileged. "[Our] mom made us feel like we had everything we needed," he said. "We knew we weren't rich, but we never felt like we were poor." In his 2006 autobiography, *Touchdown Alexander,* he cited his favorite childhood memories as the annual Christmas celebrations at his grandparents' house. Everyone was made to feel welcome at these gatherings, and many gifts were exchanged. "I grew up with that sense of being a family and loving one another. For me, Christmas wasn't about presents, it was about family—our large and loving family."

Alexander's mother has always been a positive influence on his life. She was caring and loving toward her sons, but also insisted they they learn to be polite, respectful, and tidy. "Looking back, it was to my advantage to have a mother like that," he recalled. "She was the queen of discipline. She kept things very strict in our home. . . . But Mom balanced her disci-

Alexander shares a laugh with his mother, Carol Alexander, following practice.

pline with love." Among many other lessons, his mother taught him the importance of integrity of character and self-discipline. "I am who I am because I had a wise mother, who not only took me to church . . . but has lived the life she taught me to live," he affirmed.

As a boy, Alexander attended St. Stephen's Missionary Baptist Church in Cincinnati. He remembers being awestruck by the lively and inspiring sounds of the gospel choir, but admits that he did not pay much attention to the preaching until he was about 10 years old. After experiencing an emotionally uplifting worship service in the spring of 1987, though, he elected to become a baptized member of the church. His mother and pastor both encouraged him to make a spiritual pledge to live according to the principles of his Christian faith. Since the day he joined the church, he has strived to be obedient to its teachings. "Very early I learned that we make choices," he explained in his autobiography. "We have to choose which path we will follow—we have to choose to love, to forgive, and to enjoy being alive. And we show we've decided by the way we live."

First Taste of Football

Durran and Shaun were virtually inseparable throughout their childhoods. Whether playing make-believe games in their living room or tossing a football in a field behind their apartment building, they could almost always be found together. Although they were only a year apart in age, Shaun looked up to Durran as a role model and father figure. Even today, he rarely makes an important decision without consulting his brother first, and the two have a longstanding ritual of talking by phone before every game.

Today, Alexander credits his older brother with setting a great example, both in academics and sports. "He set the pattern for me," Alexander explained. It was only after much prodding from his brother, for example, that Alexander agreed to become a member of the pee wee football team that Durran had joined. He found that while he liked playing football, he especially liked the post-game pizza parties. "And that," he said, "was my start in playing football—when I was still more interested in the pizza and fun with friends than in the game itself."

Alexander started his pee wee career in third grade as a defensive end. His coach made him a kick returner the following year. He returned two kickoffs for touchdowns in the first game of the season. Delighted by the cheers and attention he received after each return, he approached Durran after the game and asked him which position scored the most points. When Durran revealed that the running back made the most touchdowns, Shaun decided to switch positions and concentrate his efforts on scoring. By sixth grade, his family, coaches, and teammates all recognized that he possessed a special talent for carrying the football. "When people saw Shaun in Pee Wee," his father recalled, "everyone said the same thing: 'That kid's going to play [college football] on Saturdays.'"

EDUCATION

Alexander attended Florence Elementary School, where he was usually identified by teachers as "Durran's younger brother" because of Durran's straight-A record. He admired his brother and tried to emulate him, but often felt he could not match Durran's accomplishments. Finally, in sixth grade, his teacher offered some words of wisdom that changed his perspective. "[You] don't have to be like Durran. You just have to be the best Shaun the world's ever seen," she advised. From that day on, he stopped comparing himself to Durran and focused instead on doing his best.

Alexander focused on business before setting his sights on an athletic career. His favorite subject was algebra, and he often talked about someday becoming an important business leader. By high school, his leadership qualities were on full display. He was elected president of his class at Boone County High School every year from ninth through 12th grade. He also balanced academics and athletics with ease, posting a 3.5 grade point average even as he starred in basketball, baseball, and football for the Boone County High School Rebels.

In his junior year, Alexander was asked to replace the varsity football team's injured first-string tailback. His first game as the Rebels' starting running back was a memorable one. "My first carry in the game was a touchdown," he remembered. "So was my second. At halftime, I had 214 yards rushing and four touchdowns." Later in the game, an opponent tackled him so hard that Alexander bit through his own lip. Alexander still has a scar under his chin from the incident—the only lasting scar he has ever received in all of his years of football.

By the end of his junior year, Alexander had tallied an astounding 2,400 yards rushing and 42 touchdowns. At the conclusion of the season, head coach Mike Murphy, told him: "You'll go to a big college, and you'll play in the pros. You're going to have an outstanding career, Shaun." Until this point, Alexander had never really viewed football as a career path. But his coach's words made him realize that he had a special gift for the game.

Alexander was even more dominant as a high school senior. He led his team to its second 4A state championship in three seasons with an incredible tally of 54 touchdowns and 3,500 rushing yards. On two occasions, he scored seven touchdowns in one game. Alexander received national recognition for these gridiron exploits. He was selected as a *Parade* magazine and *USA Today* All-American, and was designated "Old Spice Athlete of the Month" by *Sports Illustrated,* which nicknamed him "Mr. Touchdown." He became known as "Alexander the Great" to high school football fans throughout the region and was honored as the Gatorade Circle of Champions Kentucky Player of the Year. Boone County High School even retired his number 37 jersey at a special ceremony staged a few weeks before his graduation.

> *"My friends and I would rule out schools because we didn't like their uniforms," Alexander recalled. "That was the first step. The second step was a screening committee that included my brother, my cousin and our best friend. If we didn't like a recruiter, we crossed that school off the list."*

Alexander's incredible high school career attracted the attention of major college football programs across the country. He eventually narrowed his choices down to the University of Michigan, the University of Alabama, and Notre Dame, where Durran played drums in the marching band. "My friends and I would rule out schools because we didn't like their uniforms," he joked as he described the difficult selection process. "That was the first step. The second step was a screening committee that included my brother, my cousin and our best friend. If we didn't like a recruiter, we crossed that school off the list." After visiting all three schools under consideration, he chose to accept a scholarship from the Alabama Crimson Tide because of the school's warm-weather location and the enthusiasm of the students.

Alexander began his studies at the University of Alabama in the fall of 1995. He graduated with a bachelor's degree in marketing in 1999. As a college senior, he garnered Academic All-SEC (Southeastern Conference) honors for maintaining a grade point average of 3.0 or above.

CAREER HIGHLIGHTS

Playing for the Alabama Crimson Tide

Alabama coaches "redshirted" Alexander during his freshman year. This designation allowed him to practice with the team throughout the season without using any of the four years of athletic eligibility allotted to college players. As a "redshirt freshman" the following year, he began the season as the team's third-string tailback. But late in the season, in a game against archrival Louisiana State University (LSU), Alexander burst into the spotlight and launched one of the greatest careers in Crimson Tide history.

Alexander began the game against the LSU Tigers on the bench, as usual. But late in the first half he entered the game and promptly rambled for a 17-yard touchdown run. On the first drive after half-time, he raced 72 yards for a second touchdown. By the end of the game, Alexander had scored a third touchdown and posted a single-game school record of 291 yards rushing to lead the Crimson Tide to victory. He finished the 1996 campaign with 589 rushing yards and six touchdowns. His surprising contributions helped lift Alabama to a solid 10-3 record for the year.

The 1997 season was a difficult one for Alexander and the Crimson Tide. Injuries dogged Alexander, who managed only 415 rushing yards and three touchdowns for the year. The team, meanwhile, posted only four wins all season long. In 1998, though, both Alexander and the Tide rebounded. The star tailback cruised to 17 touchdowns (13 rushing and four receiving) and gained 1,178 yards rushing to help guide Alabama to a

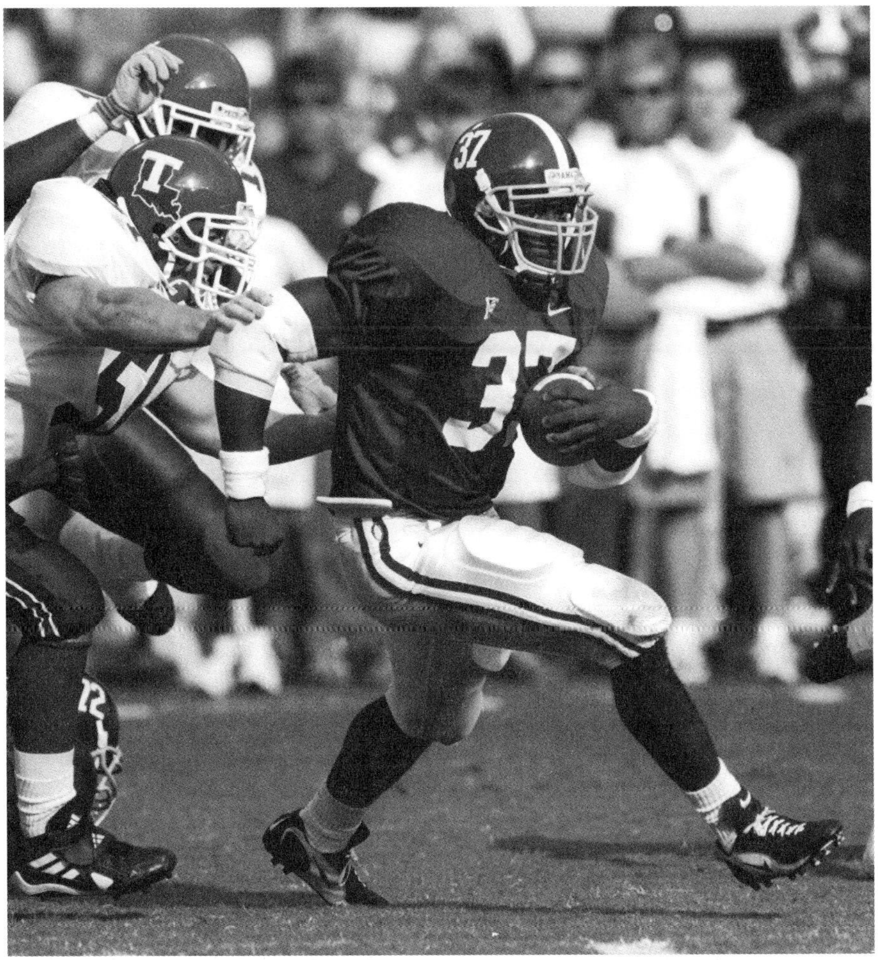

During his years at the University of Alabama, Alexander set a host of school rushing records.

winning record (7-5). His performance earned him All-Southeast Conference honors at season's end.

As his senior year approached, Alexander was a local celebrity and the team's star player. He proved worthy of all the attention during the 1999 season. He shredded opposing defenses to rack up 1,383 rushing yards and 23 touchdowns (including 19 on the ground) despite missing three games with an ankle injury. Alexander's performance earned him SEC Offensive Player of the Year honors and helped lift the Crimson Tide to a 10-3 record and conference championship. The two most memorable victories of the season came against the Florida Gators. Early in the season, Alexander and his teammates snapped Florida's 30-game winning streak in a 40-39 thriller. Two months later, the Crimson Tide rolled over the Gators by a 34-7 score to win the conference championship.

Alexander ended his career with the Crimson Tide with a number of SEC records. He also left Alabama with 15 school records, including a school-best 3,565 career rushing yards. If he had not suffered his ankle injury, many observers believe that he would have been a serious contender for the 1999 Heisman Trophy, the prize awarded to the year's most outstanding college football player. But Alexander refused to dwell on what might have been. "We all set goals and sometimes barely miss them," he said. "Don't be depressed. Instead, be thankful for where you are. Use the near misses as fuel for later success."

"

"We all set goals and sometimes barely miss them," Alexander said. "Don't be depressed. Instead, be thankful for where you are. Use the near misses as fuel for later success."

"

Joining the Seattle Seahawks

In the first round of the 2000 National Football League draft, the Seattle Seahawks chose Alexander as the 19th overall pick. Many had predicted that the 5'11" and 225 pound running back would be selected sooner, even though he was neither the biggest nor the fastest running back available. For his part, Alexander quietly decided to prove that the teams that had passed him over had made a major error.

When Alexander joined the Seahawks, he was slotted behind Ricky Watters, the team's veteran tailback. Watters taught him valuable lessons, including how to avoid the crushing hit and how to respond to the long grind of an NFL season. "It turned out to be a great blessing to be mentored by one of the greatest running backs of the 1990s," Alexander later said. He played in all 16 games of his rookie season, functioning primarily as the team's short-yardage back on third and fourth downs. He scored his first professional touchdown against the Kansas City Chiefs in a game that likewise marked his first career start. Although he saw limited action in his rookie season, his 4.9 yards-per-carry average was the second highest among first-year NFL running backs.

Alexander's second season marked his emergence as an NFL star. When Watters suffered a serious shoulder injury early in the season, the former

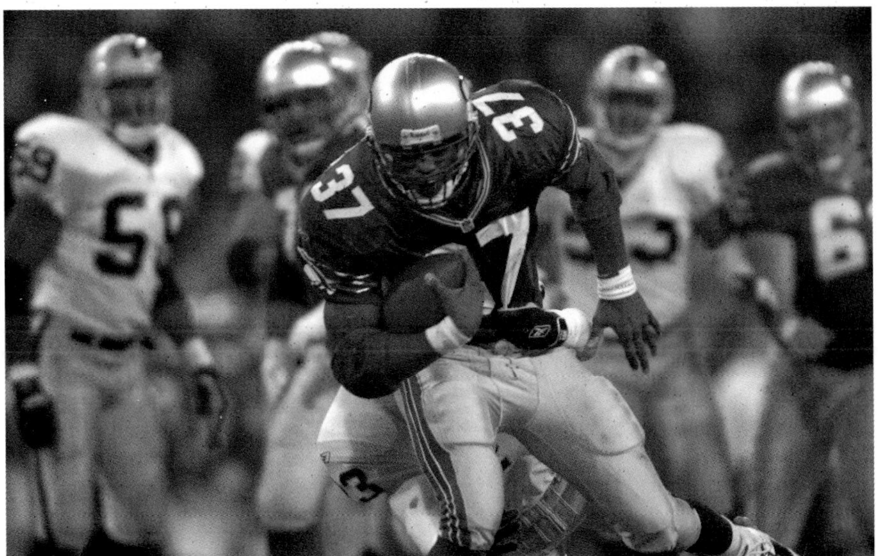

In this November 2001 game against the Oakland Raiders, Alexander rushed for 266 yards on 35 carries.

Crimson Tide star found himself in the starting lineup. He made the most of the opportunity, wracking up big yardage in nearly every game. Alexander had a particularly monumental game in November against the Oakland Raiders. In his most productive game to date, he scored three touchdowns and rushed for 266 yards on 35 carries—the fourth-best single-game total in NFL history and a franchise record. His offensive performance in that game, which included an 88-yard touchdown run, earned him recognition as the American Football Conference Player of the Week. "Shaun has gotten better with his decision-making each week. He is becoming much more aware, and a much better situational runner than he was at the beginning of the year," said Head Coach Mike Holmgren after the game.

Despite only starting in 12 games during the 2001 season, Alexander led the NFL with 14 rushing touchdowns. He finished the year with 1,318 yards on 309 attempts, the fifth-highest rushing total in the history of the team. Following the 2001 season, he was hired by the Fox Sports network to host a short-lived variety show, *Shaun Alexander Live.* In it, the writers often poked fun at Alexander's lack of recognition among fans despite his accomplishments on the field. The Christmas special, for example, included a skit set in Seattle's Factoria Mall that opened with the line: "Santa, I think all I want this year for Christmas is some people to recognize me."

Superstar in Seattle

Watters retired at the end of the 2001 season, leaving Alexander as Seattle's undisputed backfield star entering the 2002 season. Once again, Alexander proved that he could carry the team on his broad shoulders. On September 29, 2002, for example, he scored a career- and franchise-record five touchdowns in one game against the Minnesota Vikings. Moreover, he scored all five touchdowns before the end of the second quarter, which set the NFL record for touchdowns in a single half. Alexander finished the 2002 season as the National Football Conference (NFC) leader in both rushing touchdowns (16) and overall touchdowns scored (18). (The Seahawks had switched from the AFC to the NFC prior to the 2002 campaign.)

——— " ———

When Alexander angrily criticized his coach in a post-game outburst, he ignited a storm of controversy. He apologized for his comments two days later. "I'm human," he confessed. "Anybody can, at one time, pop off. And I've done it several times. I'm not worried about my image."

In 2003 Alexander tallied 16 touchdowns and a career-best 1,435 yards. This performance resulted in his first invitation to play in the Pro Bowl, the NFL's all-star game. He earned his second trip to the Pro Bowl in 2004 after recording a career-best 1,696 yards rushing (second best in the NFL) and an NFL-best 20 total touchdowns. The Seahawks qualified for the NFC playoffs in both 2003 and 2004, but lost in the first round on both occasions.

The end of the 2004 season also was marred by the first negative publicity of Alexander's career. He entered the final week of the season in a neck-and-neck duel with Curtis Martin of the New York Jets for the league rushing title. After both teams finished their last games, Alexander trailed Martin by a single yard. When the Seahawks star learned this, he angrily criticized Head Coach Mike Holmgren for ordering a quarterback sneak on the team's last offensive play — even though it resulted in a division crown-clinching touchdown. Alexander even claimed that Holmgren had "stabbed him in the back" by failing to call a running play for him.

Alexander's post-game outburst ignited a storm of controversy. Stung by accusations that he was just another selfish, pampered athlete, Alexander apologized for his comments two days later. "I'm human," he confessed.

"Anybody can, at one time, pop off. And I've done it several times. I'm not worried about my image." But he also claimed that his remarks were blown out of proportion. "You take any story, and you can get confused. You can make the bad guy look like the good guy. You can make Cinderella look like the wicked stepsister. . . . That's just reality. I understand that," he said.

Alexander proudly accepts the 2005 NFL Most Valuable Player trophy.

Since the 2004 incident, Alexander has repeatedly praised Holmgren's leadership of the team. "[He is] a man of enormous confidence . . . [who] instills that same confidence in the rest of us," Alexander declared. Before training camp in 2005, he signed a one-year, $6.32 million contract with Seattle that included an option for him to become an unrestricted free agent at the season's end.

Advancing to the Super Bowl

In 2005 Alexander helped guide the Seattle Seahawks to the most successful season in franchise history. Described by Dennis Dillon of the *Sporting News* as "the NFL's most underappreciated, underrated and underexposed superstar," Alexander won the NFL rushing title with 1,880 yards. In addition, his 28 total touchdowns set a new single-season NFL record in that category. On January 5, 2006, he was named Most Valuable Player in the NFL, and was recognized as the Associated Press Offensive Player of the Year the following day. He joined the ranks of Emmitt Smith, Priest Holmes, and Marshall Faulk as one of few tailbacks in NFL history to enjoy back-to-back seasons of 20 or more touchdowns, and became the only player to achieve at least 15 touchdowns for five consecutive years. He also became the first Seahawk in team history to be featured on the cover of *Sports Illustrated.*

More importantly, Alexander's terrific play was the single greatest factor in Seattle's 13-3 division-winning regular season mark. The Seahawks then toppled the Washington Redskins in the divisional playoffs.

Alexander, however, suffered what the *Seattle Post-Intelligencer* termed a "franchise-chilling concussion" 10 minutes into the first quarter. He missed the rest of the Washington game, but returned to the field the following weekend for the conference championship game. He churned out 132 rushing yards to set a team playoff record and scored two touchdowns to lift the Seahawks over the Carolina Panthers. This triumph put the Seahawks in Super Bowl XL to face the AFC champion Pittsburgh Steelers. "It hasn't sunk in yet that we're one game away from being legendary," he admitted following the win.

In the days leading up to the big Super Bowl clash, the Steelers made it clear that their top defensive priority was to shut down Alexander. "He can run you over," Steelers safety Troy Polamalu explained. "He has speed, agility and an ability to make people miss. I think his combination is far above anybody else."

"

"If it doesn't feel right to do—even though I can't explain the reason—I don't do it," Alexander declared. "When you know what's right and wrong, all you have to do is make that decision to do right, avoid wrong—and follow through."

"

As Super Bowl XL unfolded, it became clear that Pittsburgh could not completely neutralize Seattle's talented running back. Alexander rumbled for a team-high 95 yards on 20 tough carries. But despite his success on the ground, the Steelers claimed a 21-10 victory. Afterwards, Alexander tried to explain the mixed emotions he felt about his Super Bowl experience. "I was sad we had lost so badly, but I had joy in the midst of disappointment," he said. "*I had actually played at the Super Bowl.*"

"Alexander the Great"

Following his stellar 2005 season, Alexander had claimed virtually every major Seahawks career rushing record. He finished the year with 7,817 cumulative rushing yards and an amazing 100 touchdowns (89 rushing and 11 receiving) in his six seasons with the team. Accordingly, reporter Bob Brookover of the *Philadelphia Inquirer* called him "probably the greatest player to ever wear a Seahawks uniform." Alexander, however, has his sights set on the NFL record for career touchdowns. "I still don't think I've had my best year," he said. "I want to win the MVP Award a second time, a third time . . . and maybe even a fourth time! Other running backs have

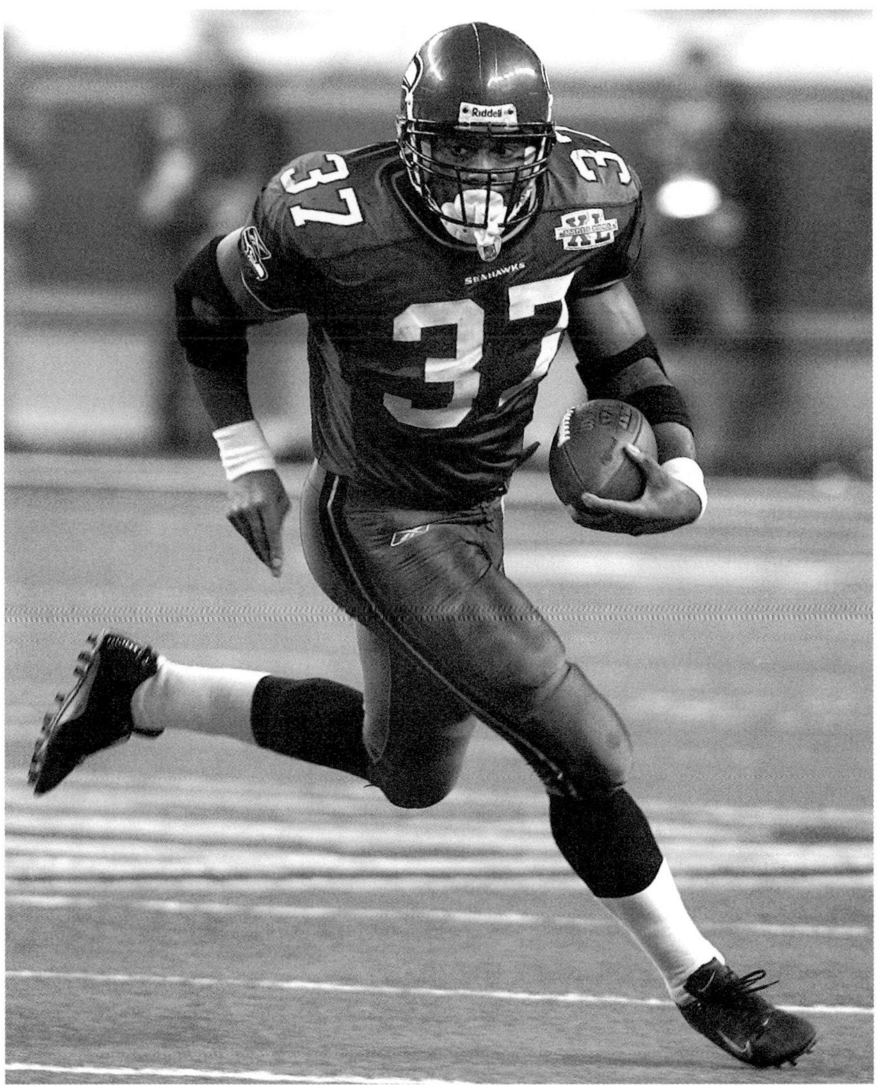

Alexander and his team suffered a disappointing 21-10 loss against the Pittsburgh Steelers in the Super Bowl, February 2006.

won it. . . . But no running back has ever won it two years in a row. I'd like to be the first to do that."

Alexander signed a $62 million, eight-year contract extension with Seattle in March 2006. Even though the agreement stood as the highest-paying contract in NFL history for a running back, Seahawks President Tim Ruskell was delighted by the deal. "We have just signed one of the best running backs in the history of the National Football League in essence to a lifetime deal," he said. "We couldn't be more excited and the team is excited and Shaun is obviously excited." Alexander described the contract as a "blessing." He added, however, that "I didn't play football for money . . . the money is not going to be what drives me. It never has and it never will."

Today, Alexander ranks as one of the most popular players in the NFL. He is featured on the cover of the *Madden NFL 07* video game, and is phenomenally popular in Florence, Kentucky, where he returns every off-season. "Yes, the kids are in awe of him when he comes back. But by the same token, he's made them feel a part of it all," Boone County High School coach Rick Thompson told the *Los Angeles Times.* In fact, Alexander telephones the coach before each of the team's Friday night football games to provide encouragement. The Florence community, meanwhile, showed their high regard for their famous native son by changing the name of a street adjacent to his old high school to Shaun Alexander Way.

In August 2006 Alexander published his autobiography, co-written with Cecil Murphey. One of his motivations for writing the book, he stated, was "to show people — especially young people — that success is closer than they may think." With this in mind, he wrote at length about his commitment to ethical principles and self-discipline and emphasized how important these factors were in his professional success. "If it doesn't feel right to do — even though I can't explain the reason — I don't do it," he stated. For example, he abstained from sex prior to marriage and has refrained from using alcohol and drugs. "When you know what's right and wrong, all you have to do is make that decision to do right, avoid wrong — and follow through."

MARRIAGE AND FAMILY

Alexander married Valerie Boyd on May 18, 2002, in Florence, Kentucky. He met Boyd the day after he arrived in Seattle to begin his NFL career at a small party hosted by a teammate. Alexander proposed to Boyd in December 2001 during a horse-drawn carriage ride through Central Park in New York City. The couple shared their first kiss, Alexander revealed in his autobiography, during their wedding ceremony. "It was worth the wait," he confirmed.

The couple's first daughter, Heaven Nashay, was born on September 21, 2003, a game day. Alexander broke his 34-game starting streak with the Seahawks to assist with the birth. "It was my first catch of the day," he told reporters. Although he missed the first quarter, he arrived in time to finish the game with 58 rushing yards. "I'll always remember that day . . . as very, very special," he said. The Alexander family expanded to include a second daughter, Trinity Monet, on July 28, 2005.

The Alexanders reside in Kirkland, Washington, where they intend to raise a large family. Valerie has disclosed that she would like nine children, and the couple has expressed an interest in adoption. The family attends the Christian Faith Center in Seattle, a nondenominational, Bible-based church. As the player attests in the opening paragraph of *Touchdown Alexander,* "[Football is] what I *do,* but that's not who I *am.* . . . I'm also a husband, a father, and a Christian man. I'm a mentor to younger men as well, because they are our future."

HOBBIES AND OTHER INTERESTS

Alexander likes to play basketball and golf in his spare time. While on the road, he often plays cards with fellow team members. His favorite television show is "American Idol," and he also regularly watches college basketball games. His favorite actor is Eddie Murphy, and he knows all of the lines to his favorite Murphy film, *Coming to America.* He also listens to gospel music and cites Ruben Studdard and Kirk Franklin as his favorite recording artists.

"[Football is] what I do, but that's not who I am. . . . I'm also a husband, a father, and a Christian man. I'm a mentor to younger men as well, because they are our future."

Alexander also is pursuing his lifelong interest in business and advertising, and envisions himself running a real estate or marketing company following his NFL career. "I will have a few business things that will be more lucrative than the business I'm in right now," he has predicted.

Finally, Alexander sees himself as a philanthropist dedicated to the betterment of the community. He has volunteered time to such organizations as the Fellowship of Christian Athletes, and in 2000 he founded the nonprofit Shaun Alexander Foundation to help young men develop leadership skills and integrity. "This is a fatherless generation," he explained. "Young men are not taught that they're important. We're not taught how to be men, how to make decisions or how to fight for what is correct." The mission of the organization is to encourage youngsters to reach their potential as mentors and role models through education, athletics, character-building, and leadership programs. For example, the foundation offers a session for middle-school age boys that, according to Alexander, "teaches them the values of staying in school and making wise decisions with money." It even sponsors a chess-playing program for children in the second and third grades.

When asked about his interest in extensive charity work, Alexander has explained that "that's how my mother was, and pretty much how my family is. So I was taught that. Now I'm just in a higher-income level, so we just give a little more." Alexander's efforts on behalf of those less fortunate than himself has caught the attention of other community-oriented NFL players, such as New England Patriot fullback Heath Evans. "For both of us, [football] is more a means to an end," Evans revealed. "We have a heart for kids, especially Shaun. He spends his off-season speaking to youth groups and youth rallies. I think that's Shaun's true passion."

HONORS AND AWARDS

High School All-American (*Parade; USA Today*): 1995
SEC Player of the Year (SEC Coaches): 1999
NFC Pro Bowl Team: 2003-05
Bert Bell Award (Maxwell Football Club): 2005, Professional American Football Player of the Year
ESPY Award (ESPN): 2005, Best NFL Player
NFL Most Valuable Player Award (Associated Press): 2005
NFL Offensive Player of the Year (Associated Press): 2005
NFL Rushing Title: 2005

FURTHER READING

Books

Alexander, Shaun, with Cecil Murphey. *Touchdown Alexander,* 2006
Mentink, Jarrett. *Alexander the Great,* 2004 (juvenile)

Periodicals

Men's Fitness, Dec. 2005, p.50
New York Post, Feb. 6, 2006, Metro section, p.89
Seattle Post-Intelligencer, Nov. 22, 2001, p.D1; Dec. 25, 2002, p.C1; Oct. 22, 2003, p.D8; Aug. 24, 2006, p.D2
Seattle Times, Jan. 4, 2005, p.D1; Jan. 8, 2006, p.D1; July 30, 2006, p.C2
Sporting News, Dec. 23, 2005, p.18

Sports Illustrated, Jan. 10, 2005, p.28; Dec. 19, 2005, p.46
Sports Illustrated KIDS, Mar. 2005, p.53; Sep. 2006, p.26

Online Articles

http://www.nfl.com/news/archive/01/2006
(NFL.com Wire Reports, "Alexander Ready to Go for NFC Championship," Jan. 18, 2006)
http://www.nfl.com/news/archive/02/2006
(NFL.com Wire Reports, "MVP Alexander Considers Seahawks, Others," Feb. 12, 2006)
http://www.nfl.com/news/archive/04/2006
(NFL News, "Alexander Selected for *Madden '07* Cover," Apr. 21, 2006)

Online Databases

Biography Resource Center Online, 2007

ADDRESS

Shaun Alexander
Seattle Seahawks
11220 N.E. 53rd Street
Kirkland, WA 98033

WORLD WIDE WEB SITES

http://www.nfl.com
http://www.rolltide.com
http://www.seahawks.com
http://www.shaunalexander.org

Chris Brown 1989-

American R&B Singer and Actor
Creator of the Popular Songs "Run It" and "Yo (Excuse Me Miss)"

BIRTH

Christopher Maurice Brown was born on May 5, 1989, in Tappahannock, Virginia, a small town with a population of about 2,000. His mother, Joyce Hawkins, operated a daycare center, and his father, Clinton Brown, worked as a corrections officer at a prison. Brown recalled that his father was tough on the inmates, "but to me he was always real lenient, letting me get away with a lot of stuff." Brown has an older sister, Lytrell Bundy, who works in a bank.

YOUTH

Brown grew up in a family that loved music. Through his parents' music collection, he became familiar with R&B and pop singers of past and present eras, including Sam Cooke, Stevie Wonder, Michael Jackson, Anita Baker, and Aretha Franklin. Brown began dancing in front of the television at home as a small child. "When I was two," he recalled, "I knew I was bound to do something in entertainment. I was dancing and watching TV and seeing people like Michael Jackson. It just came to me, and from that point on, I was always dancing." However, it was not until his mother heard him singing along with Usher's "My Way" when he was 11 years old that she realized her son had an undeniable talent. "My mom was like, 'You can sing?' And I was like, 'Well, yeah, Mama.'"

"It's funny: I miss my public school, because in public school you can take your test and get your work done but you're around your friends and girls, and that way you're more influenced to do [your work] instead of just being with one tutor by yourself."

EDUCATION

Brown attended Essex High School in Tappahannock until early 2005, when he moved to the New York area to pursue a music career. Since that time he has been home schooled and still travels with a tutor. On his web site he lists his favorite school subjects as math and biology. Public appearances and media interviews are scheduled around his school day so they do not interfere with his education. Brown has said that he sometimes misses his old school, which had about 500 students. "It's funny: I miss my public school, because in public school you can take your test and get your work done but you're around your friends and girls, and that way you're more influenced to do [your work] instead of just being with one tutor by yourself." Brown's manager, Tina Davis, said that "his education is just as important to us, so he goes to school every morning, even Saturdays and Sundays."

CAREER HIGHLIGHTS

Getting Started

Brown enjoyed singing for his friends and girls at school but did not do so professionally until his father met a talent agent by chance at a local gas station. Soon Brown began recording songs with a production team in Richmond, Virginia, about 45 miles from his home. He was 13 years old. He later connected with a songwriter and producer in New York and traveled there with his mother to audition for a recording contract with a national label.

Brown was ecstatic when he heard his song "Run It!" on the radio for the first time. "I was actually at my house in New Jersey, and [radio station] Hot 97 played the record. I was just real excited. I knew it was my record when I first heard the beat, so I ran upstairs and told my mom, 'Ma, it's on, it's on, it's on!' So it was just crazy."

In August 2004 he met Tina Davis, who was then vice president of A&R (Artists and Repertoire) for Def Jam Records, which included the artists Jay-Z, Ludacris, and LL Cool J. A&R executives like Davis scout and develop new talent. Davis was enthusiastic about Brown's potential and so was company president L.A. Reid, who had helped launch the careers of such well-known acts as TLC and Usher in the 1990s. However, before a deal could be finalized, Davis left Def Jam. She became Brown's business manager, and under her guidance he signed instead with Jive Records. Jive is part of the Zomba Label Group, which includes such top-selling performers as Justin Timberlake and R. Kelly.

Brown spent the next few months recording songs for his first album. He worked with several highly sought after songwriters and producers, including Sean Garrett and Scott Storch ("Gimme That," "Run it!" featuring Juelz Santana), Vidal Davis and Andre Harris ("Yo [Excuse Me Miss]"), Jermaine Dupri ("Run It!" Remix featuring Bow Wow and Jermaine Dupri), and Bryan Michael Cox ("Say Goodbye"). Altogether Brown recorded about 50 songs, only 15 of which would be chosen for the CD. (The rest are reserved for later release, possibly on movie soundtracks or on a subsequent album.) Brown has said that the songs selected for the album were chosen specifically to reflect age-appropriate themes for a teenage performer, including hanging out with friends, meeting girls, and

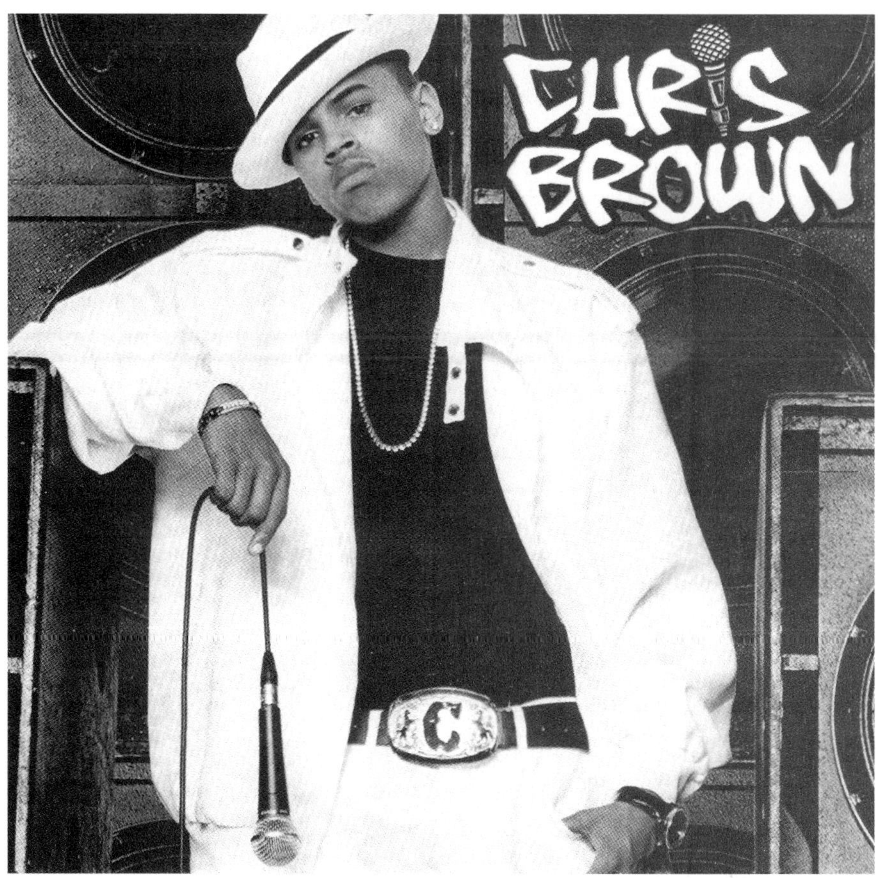

falling in love. "I'm young," he explained on his web site. "I want to appeal to people my age as well as older people. This gives me time to grow with my audience."

Releasing "Run It!"

Brown's debut single, "Run It!" featuring rapper Juelz Santana, was released on July 26, 2005. Brown was ecstatic when he heard the song on the radio for the first time. "I was actually at my house in New Jersey, and [radio station] Hot 97 played the record. I was just real excited. I knew it was my record when I first heard the beat, so I ran upstairs and told my mom, 'Ma, it's on, it's on, it's on!' So it was just crazy." The video for "Run It," which was nominated for an MTV Music Award in 2006, showcases Brown as both a singer and dancer. In the video, teenagers climb through a window into a school gym at night and hold an impromptu dance. The boys and girls face off in groups, each showing their dance moves. Brown's dancing wins the interest of his beautiful counterpart, but both groups scatter when security guards arrive. Interviewed on his web site, Brown said that he came up with the concept for the video because he "just wanted to bring to the kids and everybody just dancing, the whole feel of dancing. . . . Sneaking away and going into this abandoned school and just gettin' off, doing what you gotta do—dance, holler at girls, the girls holler at you."

"

Brown said that he came up with the concept for the "Run It!" video because he "just wanted to bring to the kids and everybody just dancing, the whole feel of dancing. . . . Sneaking away and going into this abandoned school and just gettin' off, doing what you gotta do—dance, holler at girls, the girls holler at you."

The release of his self-titled debut CD, *Chris Brown,* was planned for fall 2005. But first, Jive Records sent Brown out on a tour to make personal appearances around the country. He visited schools and malls, posing for photographs and signing autographs for many young fans. With his good looks, fashion sense, and personal charm, Brown quickly established a large female fan base. He also made a favorable impression on the industry insiders who would support his career. According to Colby Colb, a radio programming director in Philadelphia, "I was taken aback by the fact that he was willing to sign autographs for three hours. But that's the key to his appeal: He's like a regular guy who gets the whole star thing but isn't diva-fied yet. He's very humble."

By late November 2005, "Run It!" was the *Billboard* Hot 100 No. 1 single in the United States, holding that position for five weeks. It topped the *Billboard* Pop 100 chart as well, and remained in the top spot throughout the holidays and into January 2006. Meanwhile, Brown's CD, *Chris Brown,* debuted in the No. 2 position on the *Billboard* 200 hot album list in late November. In its first week of sales the CD sold 155,000 copies. During the same week, "Run It!" was downloaded more than five million times, according to Jeff Leeds in the *New York Times*. Jive Records vice president Lisa Cambridge commented on the quick success of Brown's first release. "We did [a music] industry showcase last May in front of 300 people. That was the first time he'd ever been onstage, singing into a microphone,"

Cambridge said. "Chris went from singing in front of the mirror in his bedroom to having the No. 1 [single] in the country."

Showing off his dance moves on MTV's "Total Request Live"(TRL).

Krumping

Brown's second single, "Yo (Excuse Me Miss)" was released in February 2006. The video for the song features Brown and two companions dancing down the sidewalk in pursuit of a gorgeous girl he glimpsed through a shop window. Brown dances in what is known as the krump style. Krump is a high-energy, acrobatic form of hip-hop dance that evolved in south central Los Angeles—in part as an alternative to street violence. Brown described krumping as "a new style, more aggressive dancing, releasing anger, releasing stress." It fuses funk and hip-hop styles from the 1970s through the 1990s with mock fighting postures. Among the styles it draws on are *popping,* which involves quickly contracting and relaxing muscles to create jerking movements, and *locking,* which combines rapid hand and arm movements with a relaxed lower body. Lockers include quick collapses to one or both knees, interact with the audience, and frequently incorporate props (such as a hat) into their routines. Many reviewers raved about Brown's dancing, comparing him to such innovative dancers as Michael Jackson and Usher. Commentator Melissa Ruggieri, for example, called his dancing "phenomenal, a nonstop blur of airborne sneakers and rubbery limbs."

Brown found success with other singles from the *Chris Brown* CD. "Gimme That" peaked at No. 15 on the Hot 100 chart, and "Say Goodbye" hit the *Billboard* Hot R&B/Hip Hop chart in November 2006. Both singles were supported by memorable videos. In "Gimme That," Brown falls asleep in a crowded modern train station and is transported in a dream to the same station in the 1920s. He sings and dances in an attempt to impress a beautiful older woman. The single and video feature rapper Lil' Wayne, who introduces Brown as "the 16-year-old phenom, Chris Breezy." Soon the nickname was picked up in the media and on the web by fans around the world.

In the confessional ballad "Say Goodbye," Brown searches for the right way to break up with a girl after he meets someone new. He sings: "How do you let it go? When you, / You just don't know? What's on, / The other side of the door / When you're walking out, talk about it / Girl I hope you understand / What I'm tryin' to say. / We just can't go on / Pretending that we get along." "Say Goodbye" became Brown's third single to reach the top ten on the *Billboard* Hot 100 Chart.

Relating to Teens

Themes of romance, desire, and disappointment echo throughout the songs on *Chris Brown*. In "Ya Man Ain't Me," Brown addresses a girl hoping to convince her to leave her current boyfriend to be with him. "Winner" uses a boxing analogy to describe how he feels knocked out by a beautiful girl he has met. Discussing in particular the song "Young Love" on his web site, he explained, "Even when teenagers really are in love with each other a lot of older people are like 'Love? You're barely old enough to go outside at night!' But what they don't know is that kids our age really do have feelings for each other, so this song is basically telling older people that even though we're young, we still love each other. I think all the teenagers can relate to it." Brown's favorite song on the CD is the final one, "Thank You." As he explained, "I wrote the whole song, really, just basically thanking my fans." In it he sings, "Thank you, you mean so much to me, / I don't know what to do / (For you and you and you and you and you and you) / Thank you from my heart right to my soul."

"[When] you dance and sing, everybody's gonna compare you to Usher or Michael. I see myself as a totally different artist," Brown once said. "I just want to be recognized as being my own person and as being a unique artist in the game."

”

Because of his youth, his innovative dance moves, and his smooth vocals, Brown has often been compared to his predecessors Michael Jackson and Usher. And, like them, Brown has been embraced by legions of female fans, making him one of today's hottest teen idols. Reviewer Melissa Ruggieri described his voice in the *Richmond Times Dispatch* as "a respectable blend of Michael Jackson falsetto and Usher heftiness." Responding to such comparisons, Brown said, "[When] you dance and sing, everybody's gonna compare you to Usher or Michael. I see myself as a totally different artist, equally unique,"

Brown once said. "I just want to be recognized as being my own person and as being a unique artist in the game."

In June 2006 the DVD *Chris Brown's Journey* was released. The disc includes a 25-minute documentary showing footage of his tour stops in Japan and England. It also contains performance footage, outtakes, videos, and "making of" segments for "Gimme That," "Yo (Excuse Me Miss)," and "Run It!"

In August 2006 Brown set off on a 29-city U.S. tour with R&B singer Ne-Yo, the girl group Cherish, and the rappers Lil' Wayne, Dem Franchize Boyz, and Juelz Santana. In addition to the songs from his debut CD, Brown's show included a medley of the Michael Jackson hits "Rock with You," "Billie Jean," and "Wanna Be Startin' Somethin.'" For these numbers he wore one sequined glove in a tribute to Jackson's signature look from the 1980s. Brown's wardrobe on stage featured a variety of looks, ranging from streetwear for "Run It!" to a three-piece white suit for the show's opening number "Gimme That." Throughout the show Brown created excitement with his remarkable dance moves. According to music reviewer David Lindquist, "Brown moved in ways that freshly combined leaping, spinning, gliding, stop-action and slow-motion."

Heading in New Directions

For Brown, the success of his music career is only the beginning. "I wanna be a mogul. . . . I wanna be a singer, actor, entrepreneur, have a clothing line, be an executive everything." The young star has already begun pursuing an acting career. Brown joined the cast of the hit television show "The O.C." for several episodes in 2006-07, the show's final season. He played Will Tutt, a lonely band geek who becomes friends with Kaitlin Cooper (played by Willa Holland). "I play, like, a band geek—I'm really stepping out of my own character," he said. "I was kind of a geek in school. . . . But [on the show] I'm geeked out all the way. I'm just trying to

Brown with Columbus Short in Stomp the Yard.

be myself and then be the character [the role calls for]. I don't look at it like this role takes away from who I am." After filming his first TV appearances, Brown confided that "I'm a rookie in the [acting] game, so the nervous jitters kicked in, but I had to get over it."

Brown made his feature film debut in *Stomp the Yard* (2007). This dance movie is about DJ Williams (played by Columbus Short), a troubled kid and street dancer from Los Angeles who moves to Atlanta to attend the historically black college Truth University. There, he discovers stepping, a precise form of dance based on African-American tradition, and becomes the focal point of a fierce rivalry between two fraternities. Brown had a secondary role as DJ's younger brother, Duron.

Brown's versatility as an artist has convinced many that his success will not be short-lived. According to BET senior music director Kelly G., "There's a huge void out there. There aren't many popular teenage boys singing who can connect with teen girls. Our audience wants Chris Brown. With Usher growing up, there's a new kid on the block who can sing and dance." Those sentiments were echoed by Barry Weiss, president of the Zomba Label Group. "[Brown has the] richness of vocal tone, the million-dollar smile, the star appeal. . . . Superstars like Usher come along every 10, 15 years. Chris Brown is in that category. He's a burgeoning superstar."

The music press has greeted Brown's success enthusiastically, calling him the "new prince of pop" and the "future of R&B." He won a host of awards in 2006, including recognition at the BET Awards, the Billboard Awards, the NAACP Image Awards, the Soul Train Music Awards, and the Teen Choice Awards. Still, Brown insists that he is a normal kid. "I just try to keep the same exact way I was in Virginia. . . . I feel the need to accomplish stuff. And God will bless me if I work and can be so humble." However, he recognizes that many kids will look up to him as a role model. "I want to be a role model—to tell kids to believe they can be something when they're older. . . . That they can follow their dreams and still be good. Innocence is good."

"I want to be a role model— to tell kids to believe they can be something when they're older. . . . That they can follow their dreams and still be good. Innocence is good."

HOME AND FAMILY

Brown lives with his mother in Cliffside Park, New Jersey.

MAJOR INFLUENCES

Brown has cited Kim Burrell, Sam Cooke, Marvin Gaye, Donnie Hathaway, Michael Jackson, Usher, and Stevie Wonder as some of his musical influences.

HOBBIES AND OTHER INTERESTS

In his limited free time, Brown enjoys basketball, playing video games, drawing, and hanging out with his friends.

CREDITS

CDs

Chris Brown, 2005

TV and Movies

"One on One," 2006
"The Brandon T. Jackson Show," 2006

"The O.C.," 2006-07
Stomp the Yard, 2007

DVDs

Chris Brown's Journey, 2006

HONORS AND AWARDS

BET Awards: 2006 (two awards), Best New Artist and Viewer's Choice for "Yo (Excuse Me Miss)"
Billboard Music Awards: 2006 (three awards), Artist of the Year, Male Artist of the Year, New Artist of the Year
Image Award (NAACP): 2006, Outstanding New Artist
Soul Train Music Award: 2006, Best R&B/Soul or Rap New Artist for "Run It"
Teen Choice Award: 2006, Choice Breakout Music Artist (Male)

FURTHER READING

Periodicals

Ebony, June 2006, p.32
Indianapolis Star, Aug. 18, 2006, p.20; Aug. 19, 2006
Jet, Jan. 30, 2006, p.40; May 29, 2006, p.54
Los Angeles Times, Nov. 27, 2005, p.E46; Oct. 4, 2006, p.E3
New York Times, Mar. 9, 2006
New York Times Upfront, Nov. 28, 2005, p.6
People, Dec. 12, 2005, p.90
Richmond (VA) Times Dispatch, Dec. 25, 2005, p.H1; Aug. 22, 2006, p.C1
Sunday Times (London), Feb. 12, 2006, p.16

Online Articles

http://www.allhiphop.com/Alternatives/?ID=226
(*All Hip Hop*, "Chris Brown: New Kid on the Block," Oct. 2005)
http://www.pollstar.com/news/viewhotstar.pl?Artist=CHSBRO
(Pollstar, "Chris Brown," Feb. 20, 2006)
http://www.teenpeople.com/teenpeople/article/0,22196,1553733_2,00.shtml
(*Teen People*, "Catching Up with Chris Brown and Ne-Yo," Nov. 17, 2006)

Online Databases

Biography Resource Center Online, 2007

ADDRESS

Chris Brown
Jive Records
137-139 West 25th Street
New York, NY 10001

WORLD WIDE WEB SITES

http://www.chrisbrownworld.com
http://www.myspace.com/chrisbrown

Aaron Dworkin 1970-

American Activist, Arts Administrator, and Musician
Founder and President of the Sphinx Organization

BIRTH

Aaron Paul Dworkin was born on September 11, 1970, in Monticello, New York. His birth parents were Vaughn Moore and Audeen Moore, who decided to put their newborn son up for adoption. Aaron was adopted at two weeks of age by Barry and Susan Dworkin, who were both New York City college professors specializing in neuroscience. They also had another son. Though he did not know his birth parents as he grew up, Aaron was reunited with them as an adult and now enjoys a close relationship with them.

YOUTH

Because of the circumstances of his birth and adoption, Aaron Dworkin's upbringing was somewhat unique. His birth father was black and his birth mother was white, so he was of biracial heritage. But in his adoptive home, both of his parents were white, and he had a white older brother. Also, his adoptive parents were Jewish and taught Aaron about their religion as he grew up. "I'm black, white, Irish, Jewish," he later explained. "So I've been exposed to a lot of different perspectives on the world."

In addition, Dworkin came in regular contact with people from a wide range of races, religions, and nationalities in his hometown of New York City. This type of community is often described as "diverse"—meaning that it includes many different kinds of people. One of the positive aspects of diversity is that it can make a person more accepting of others and less likely to fear those who have a different appearance or who practice different beliefs. This was true for Dworkin, who paid little attention to such issues as skin color. "[Race] had no significance to me," he explained about his early years. "I went to school with kids of differing backgrounds. My parents were white, my brother was white, so I just really didn't understand how there was any big deal about that." The value of diversity would become very important to Dworkin later in life.

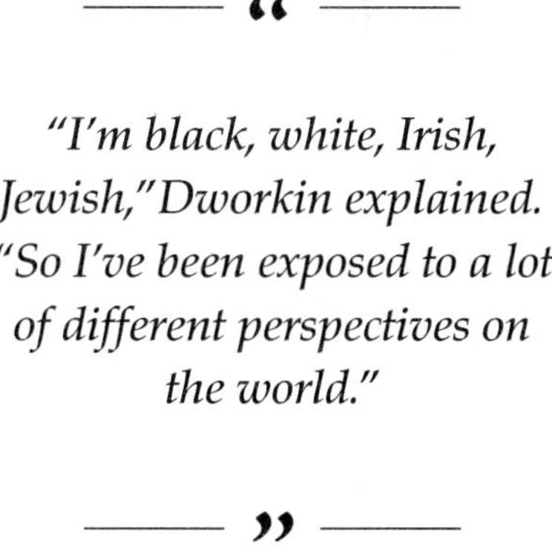
"I'm black, white, Irish, Jewish," Dworkin explained. "So I've been exposed to a lot of different perspectives on the world."

Of the many ideas and traditions that Dworkin was experienced while growing up, it was the sound of classical music that really caught his attention. His adoptive mother had been an amateur violinist before he was born. When he was about five years old, she took up her instrument once more, and the Bach compositions that she played at home excited Dworkin so much that he decided that he wanted to play too. "I thought it was the coolest thing," he said, "and so I started to play and I had a natural knack for it. It got me going pretty quick." He began formal lessons and quickly developed into a promising musician.

At age 10, Dworkin's life underwent a profound change. His family moved from Manhattan to Hershey, Pennsylvania, so that his parents could take new jobs at the Hershey Medical Center. He had to face the difficulty of enrolling in a new school and making new friends, and

Dworkin soon found that Hershey was a much different place than New York City. The most jarring change had to do with race: suddenly, his biracial heritage made him different from almost everyone else in town. "At the time, there was one black family, outside of myself, living in Hershey," he recalled. "And although it's a good town, for the first time I began to understand and grasp the feeling of racial prejudice." Certain people treated him differently because of his skin color, sometimes engaging in racist name-calling, sometimes excluding him from activities. Dworkin responded to the hostility by spending even more time immersed in his violin studies. "I used music to escape," he explained. "I could always go to my violin and play."

"I was on a downhill spiral, rebelling, feeling totally alienated," Dworkin said about his early high school years. "I felt isolated, I think, because of, you know, dating issues and being the only black kid in school and playing the violin and all these things."

EDUCATION

As a young person intent on a career in music, Dworkin took private music lessons in addition to his regular school studies. While living in Manhattan, he studied with his first teacher, the well-known violin instructor Vladimir Graffman, and in the years that followed, he studied with a long list of other accomplished musicians and music educators. He was also able to enroll in several prestigious performing arts programs, including those at the Peabody Preparatory Institute in Baltimore and the New School of Music in Philadelphia. To build his musical skills, Dworkin engaged in hours of daily practice, even though he sometimes longed for more carefree activities. As he later explained, "You want to run around with crazy kids or your friends, you don't want to practice scales or etudes."

By his teens, Dworkin was holding his own among some of the finest young musicians in the country. He performed regularly with both the Hershey Youth Orchestra and the Harrisburg Youth Symphony and attained the position of concertmaster or first violin with the Harrisburg ensemble, meaning he was judged the most skilled violinist in the orchestra. But he came to understand that race could be an issue in the musical world, just as it was elsewhere. He often found himself to be "the only

Dworkin with the Harlem Quartet after their performance at the Apollo Theater (left to right): Desmond Morris, Juan-Miguel Hernandez, Melissa White, Ilmar Gavalin, and Dworkin.

black person in every classical music situation" he encountered, and a few of his fellow musicians treated him badly because of his ethnic heritage. One of his responsibilities as concertmaster was to oversee the tuning of the instruments prior to rehearsal and performances, but some symphony members refused to cooperate. "Because I was black, they were purposefully ignoring me," he recalled.

Dworkin continued to do well in his musical activities. But by the time he reached high school, he was feeling discouraged about his life in Hershey. "I was on a downhill spiral, rebelling, feeling totally alienated," Dworkin said about his early high school years. "I felt isolated, I think, because of, you know, dating issues and being the only black kid in school and playing the violin and all these things." After completing two years at his Pennsylvania high school, his parents convinced him that he needed to try something new. It turned out to be just what he needed. "For my junior and senior year, I went to Interlochen Arts Academy, which literally saved my life." The prestigious arts school in northern Michigan, which includes a boarding school so students can live on campus, allowed Dworkin to refocus on his music. "All of a sudden I went to this place where all they really cared about was what art form you were doing and it was this utter transformation. . . . I was astounded." Interlochen also brought him in contact with a dozen or so other black arts students, which eased some of his feelings of racial isolation. Dworkin graduated from Interlochen Arts Academy in about 1988.

Dworkin then enrolled at Pennsylvania State University, where he served as concertmaster for the Penn State Philharmonic Orchestra. Rather than majoring in music, however, he studied business at the college until he withdrew without earning a degree because of financial reasons. Dworkin then moved to Michigan and spent several years working at various jobs before deciding to return to college at the University of Michigan (U-M) in the mid-1990s. There, he once more dedicated himself to his violin studies, earning his bachelor's degree (B.M.) in music in 1997 and a master's degree (M.M.) in 1998, graduating with high honors.

During his time at U-M, Dworkin began to think more carefully about the subject of race and classical music. This was partly inspired by his discovery of works of music that had been written by African-American composers, including William Grant Still. "All the time growing up as a young black violinist, I never knew there was music by black composers," he said. "I thought how could I have not known about this music?" Dworkin decided that more people—particularly young black musicians—should be exposed to this work. He also considered the fact that there were very few people of color involved with the classical music concerts where he performed. "I'd see 4,000 white faces in the audience," he remembered. "And I'd see no minorities on the stage. I wondered why there should be no place for minorities in classical music, something that was very important to me—something I loved." After spending a long time pondering the lack of racial and cultural diversity among the nation's orchestras, Dworkin asked himself an important question: "What can I do about it?"

CAREER HIGHLIGHTS

Dworkin's answer was to create the Sphinx Organization in 1996, while he was still an undergraduate at the university. This nonprofit group has been his life's work ever since. The goal of the Sphinx Organization is to increase minority participation in classical music. From his own experience, Dworkin knew that there were a limited number of black and Hispanic music students, and the numbers are even more striking on the professional level. According to most estimates, less than 4 percent of orchestral players in the United States are of either African-American or Latino heritage, even though blacks and Hispanics form about a quarter of the U.S. population. In other words, orchestras are mostly made up of white musicians, along with some members of Asian heritage. As a result, most orchestras fail to reflect the diversity that's found in the United States.

This can be bad for several reasons. First, it allows little minority input into classical music and can discourage talented minority musicians from pursuing professional careers because they feel out of place. Second, it gives some people the false idea that blacks and Hispanics aren't capable of performing classical music and that they are in some way culturally inferior. Third, with few minority musicians in the professional ranks, the larger African-American and Latino population is less likely to feel interested in classical music, which means that they often miss out on an important art form. Dworkin feels that the lack of diversity hurts the orchestras as well. Without participation from the minority population, the orchestras are out of touch with their communities, and this often contributes to the low attendance at classical concerts.

Some music authorities argue that the lack of diversity is caused by the fact that there are simply very few blacks and Hispanics who choose to study classical music and that little can be done to increase their numbers. Dworkin, however, knew that there were skilled minority musicians like himself throughout the country, even if their numbers were relatively small. He believed that if these players were given more attention and support, they could make it as professionals. To accomplish this, he came up with the idea of staging a competition that would showcase talented minority musicians, specifically strings players, and help them to develop their skills.

"I'd see 4,000 white faces in the audience," Dworkin remembered. "And I'd see no minorities on the stage. I wondered why there should be no place for minorities in classical music, something that was very important to me— something I loved."

”

Launching the Sphinx Competition

After hatching the idea for the contest, Dworkin faced a key challenge: raising money. Having worked for nonprofit groups before attending U-M, he knew that the Sphinx Organization wouldn't succeed without proper financing. He began his work by sending letters to a long list of celebrities and corporate leaders—anyone who might be able to help. Many of them ignored Dworkin's request for a contribution, but one person—James Wolfensohn, the president of the World Bank—had a much more positive reaction. "I got a letter back that basically said, 'This sounds like a great project. Here's a one-time contribution of $10,000 to help

Sphinx Competition participant Gareth Johnson playing at Carnegie Hall.

things get going,'" remembers Dworkin. "And I was like, 'This is gonna happen.'"

The first Sphinx Competition was held in 1998, and it set the basic framework that the event has followed ever since. Classically trained African-American and Latino musicians send in audition tapes that include specific musical selections. Based on these recordings, a jury of experts selects the semifinalists who get to attend the competition, which takes place in Ann Arbor and Detroit, Michigan. Early competitions featured musicians ages 13-19, and this was later adapted to include a junior division (for players up to age 17) and a senior division (ages 18-26). From the beginning, Dworkin has made sure that the jurors are very demanding in choosing the semifinalists. The young musicians are expected to be able to hold their own against the top national performers in their age group.

At the competition, the attendees perform before the jurors, and these performances are used to choose three finalists in each division. The finalists get the opportunity to play with a full orchestra in a special concert, which often features the work of minority composers. Based on these concert performances, the jurors select the winner and the second and third-place finishers. The finalists receive cash prizes, and many of them later get the opportunity to perform with various symphonies around the country. All of the semifinalists invited to Michigan are provided with a scholarship to attend a music camp later in the year. The value of the prizes and scholarships now totals more than $100,000 annually, with a top cash award of $10,000 for the first place winner in the senior division. As another feature of the program, Sphinx musicians who lack a professional-quality instrument can receive assistance in obtaining one.

Creating Connections

Though it is a contest, the Sphinx Competition is intended to create a nurturing environment rather than a competitive one. The participants spend a lot of time with one another during the week-long event and attend classes with the professionals who serve as the jury for the competition. By designing the competition in this way, Dworkin tried to make the event an educational experience and one that encourages the participants to bond with one another. By fostering a communal spirit, Dworkin hopes the young musicians will escape the type of isolation that he felt in his earlier years.

"The competition was like camp—it was so much fun," said participant Elena Urioste, who finished first in the junior division in 2003. "I pretty much forgot it was a competition the second I got there, because everyone was so nurturing and supportive. . . . They really promote the group mentality."

The participants have found this to be one of the most enjoyable aspects of the contest. "The competition was like camp—it was so much fun," said Elena Urioste, who finished first in the junior division in 2003. "I pretty much forgot it was a competition the second I got there, because everyone was so nurturing and supportive. . . . They really promote the group mentality." Another participant, Patrice Jackson, also valued the time she got to spend with other musicians. "I can't express how it is to learn that you're not alone, that there are other African Americans your age doing the same thing," she explained.

Dworkin also helps the participants connect with minorities who have already become professional musicians. This is accomplished by bringing in black and Hispanic players who are members of orchestras and chamber ensembles around the country. They form the Sphinx Orchestra, which supports the senior division finalists in their concert performance. These professionals serve as role models and teach the young musicians what it takes to succeed in the classical music world. "The Sphinx helped me be more aware of minority musicians who are excelling," noted Bryan Hernandez-Luch, "and their success has helped motivate me."

Ultimately, the Sphinx Competition aims to link talented minority musicians to the decision-makers who run the professional orchestras. The contest gives young players a chance to meet and perform for important figures in the classical music industry, and those musicians who place in the top spots often enjoy an even better showcase when they are featured in special symphony concerts throughout the United States. "The contacts are just great," explained Sphinx winner Gareth Johnson, "because you meet these very well-known and respected musicians and conductors, and they can continue to promote you throughout the years." Johnson added that, "It's not an exaggeration to say the competition changed my life. . . . It started my career."

From the beginning, Dworkin received support from some important figures in classical music. The legendary violinist Isaac Stern visited Ann Arbor during the inaugural competition in 1998 and gave free coaching sessions to Sphinx winners each year until his death in 2001. Classical stars Yo Yo Ma and Itzhak Perlman have also backed the competition. Thanks to hard work by Dworkin and his staff, the number of professional orchestras that host Sphinx winners for special performances has steadily increased, with 25 symphonies now taking part, including the well-known ensembles in Atlanta, Boston, Detroit, Baltimore, Cleveland, and St. Louis.

The organization has also had a lot of success in raising funds for its projects, which is what Dworkin calls "the biggest challenge" of his work. Such large corporations as Texaco, General Motors, Target, and American Express have supported Sphinx, as have such nonprofit organizations as the W. K. Kellogg Foundation and the National Endowment for the Arts. At times, the grants have reached into the millions, with the Bingham Trust pledging $1.5 million to Sphinx in 2005, and JPMorgan Chase offering $1 million in 2006.

Expanding the Sphinx Mission

As the financial resources of the Sphinx Organization have improved, the group has been able to begin a variety of new programs that promote its goal of increasing minority participation in classical music. To help mentor promising young musicians, Dworkin launched the Sphinx Performance Academy, a two-week summer program that takes place at Walnut Hill School near Boston. Founded in 2005, it offers intensive music education for 40 students each year who range between the ages of 12 and 18.

Other Sphinx programs focus on a broader issue: "The problem of bringing young people into classical music," to use Dworkin's own words. "For the kids to be motivated to play classical music in the first place, there has to be some connection," he explained. "They have to have heard it somewhere." Moreover, he believes that children's lives are enriched when they're exposed to the classics, regardless of whether they go on to pursue a music career. To help create interest in the music, the Sphinx Musical Encounters program arranges for participants in the competition to visit schools and to deliver other presentations and concerts. "We ask our kids to go back to their communities and be ambassadors for the music," Dworkin explained. "Because the same thing that sparked them to start [learning an instrument] is what's going to happen when they play."

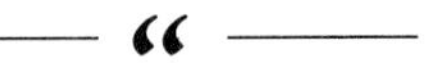

To help create interest in classical music, Sphinx arranges for participants in the competition to visit schools and to perform in concerts. "We ask our kids to go back to their communities and be ambassadors for the music," Dworkin explained. "Because the same thing that sparked them to start [learning an instrument] is what's going to happen when they play."

The organization has also developed a curriculum guide and interactive CD-ROM for use by school educators. During the 2005-2006 school year, these materials were used to teach 10,000 students about classical music. In Detroit, where Sphinx is based, the organization operates the Sphinx Preparatory Music Institute, which started in 2004. It offers introductory music classes to interested students, most whom are in middle school, and brings them together each Saturday for 20 weeks. Both the Detroit academy and the teaching materials are intended to reach children in disadvantaged urban areas. "In inner-city schools it's difficult getting kids access to good music programs," Dworkin said, because "the arts are treated as a kind of luxury" that the impoverished school districts can't afford.

These programs also help to overcome the bias that many young people have against classical music. Dworkin feels that this comes from the "stiff, sterile" way that the classics are usually presented to young people. "In that atmosphere," he said, "the last thing they will think is that classical music is fun." But when minority students get close-up exposure to the music and see it played by Sphinx contestants who share their own background, opinions often change. "It's not the music that's a barrier to young people and minorities," Dworkin argued. "When we go into schools, we find that kids just love it."

In 2004, Dworkin's organization staged the first of an ongoing series of gala concerts at Carnegie Hall in New York City. These performances, which feature winners of the Sphinx Competition, have helped reinforce the message that the Sphinx contestants possess top-level talent. In a review of the 2004 concert, a *New York Times* writer noted that "this student ensemble produced a more beautiful, precise, and carefully shaped sound than some professional orchestras that come through Carnegie Hall in the course of a year." The Carnegie concerts are yet another means of highlighting the country's skilled black and Latino classical musicians, which is all part of Dworkin's ultimate goal. "Orchestras have traditionally insisted that the minority talent simply wasn't out there," Dworkin has pointed out. "Now at least they're saying, 'Yes, the talent's there but we're not seeing those musicians at our auditions.' Getting these kids spotlighted in front of orchestras is going to change all that."

"

"Orchestras have traditionally insisted that the minority talent simply wasn't out there," Dworkin has pointed out. "Now at least they're saying, 'Yes, the talent's there but we're not seeing those musicians at our auditions.' Getting these kids spotlighted in front of orchestras is going to change all that."

"

Awards and Rewards

As the Sphinx Organization has expanded its programs, Dworkin has received increasing attention for his groundbreaking work. He was featured in the Black Entertainment Television series *History Makers in the Making* in 2003 and garnered a number of regional and national awards. Then, in September 2005, he received a phone call notifying him that he had been selected to receive one of the prestigious fellowships from the John D. and Catherine T. MacArthur Foundation. Often described as a "genius grant," a MacArthur Fellowship gives the recipient $500,000 over five years to use in any way they wish. Because the nominations for the award are kept secret, Dworkin had no idea he was being considered. "I'm rarely at a loss for

The 2006 Annual Sphinx Competition First Place Laureate, Gabriel Cabezas, with the Sphinx Chamber Orchestra.

words, but I couldn't even speak," he said of the moment when he heard that he had been selected. "Ideally this will raise the visibility of these kids," meaning the musicians in the Sphinx Competition, "because in the end it's the kids who are truly fantastic."

The year 2005 also brought about another landmark for the Sphinx Organization: three musicians who had previously been finalists in the competition landed jobs in professional orchestras, a clear sign that Dworkin's efforts were showing real results. A number of other Sphinx contestants are now enrolled in highly regarded music schools and may join the professional ranks in the near future.

Many observers believe that Dworkin has already had a big impact on the classical music world, even if the number of professional minority players still remains relatively small. "When Aaron started, you would rarely see a black or Hispanic soloist with a major orchestra," noted Steve Shipps, one of Dworkin's former professors. "Now it's become routine." The Sphinx Organization's efforts have caused symphonies and chamber-music groups to make a more determined effort to hire a more diverse group of musicians, which is likely to bring more minorities into these organizations in the coming years. Benjamin Zander, the conductor of the Boston Philharmonic, stated that "Aaron Dworkin has established—singlehandedly—the need for every classical music organization to commit to diversity."

Despite his successes, Dworkin knows that there is more work to be done. "From my perspective, we have not been successful yet, ultimately successful yet, in addressing this problem of the lack of diversity in classical music," he explained. "What I'm looking forward to is when we can go to an orchestra and there's five or ten minorities onstage, and nobody's making a big deal about it." Aaron Dworkin has vowed to continue his efforts until that mission is accomplished. "For me there really is no other option. I feel like I have to do this work," he said. "If I were to win the lottery tomorrow, I would still be doing this work and [the lottery money] would just help in making the dream come true."

——— " ———

"From my perspective, we have not been successful yet, ultimately successful yet, in addressing this problem of the lack of diversity in classical music," Dworkin explained. "What I'm looking forward to is when we can go to an orchestra and there's five or ten minorities onstage, and nobody's making a big deal about it."

HOME AND FAMILY

Dworkin met his first wife, Carrie, during his time at the Interlochen Arts Academy. The two were wed in 1997 and their son, Noah, was born in the late 1990s. They divorced in 2003, and Dworkin later married Afa Sadykhly, who serves as the vice president of programming for the Sphinx Organization. They reside in Ann Arbor, Michigan.

After seeking information about his birth parents for many years, Dworkin was able to locate them in 2001 through an adoption web site. His father, Vaughn Moore, is a hospital worker and his mother, Audeen Moore, is an emergency-management administrator. Though Vaughn and Audeen were not married when Aaron was born, they later were wed and had another child. So when Dworkin located his birth parents, he learned that he has a sister. He is on good terms with all members of his birth family and visits with them regularly.

HOBBIES AND OTHER INTERESTS

Because the Sphinx Organization quickly became a full-time job for Dworkin, he has not pursued a professional career as a musician. He has, however, continued to play violin and has recorded two CDs, *Ebony Rhythm*, which mixes classical music with dramatic readings about the historical experiences of African Americans, and *Bar-Talk*, a collaboration with his wife, Afa Sadykhly. Dworkin often plays electric violin in addition to the standard acoustic instrument, and he has developed a college-level preparatory class in electric string performance. Interested in literature as well as music, Dworkin composes poetry and has published one collection, *They Said I Wasn't Really Black*, which addresses his experiences growing up. He also founded *The Bard*, a literary magazine in Michigan, and has produced and directed a movie entitled *Deliberation*.

HONORS AND AWARDS

Alain Locke Award (The Friends of African and African-American Art): 2003
History Makers in the Making Award (Black Entertainment Television): 2003
National Governors Association Award for Distinguished Service to the Arts: 2005
John D. and Catherine T. MacArthur Foundation Fellowship: 2005
Giving Back Award (*Newsweek* magazine): 2006

FURTHER READING

Books

Contemporary Black Biography, Vol. 52, 2006

Periodicals

Chamber Music, Aug. 2006
Chronicle of Philanthropy, Oct. 27, 2005
Detroit Free Press, Feb. 7, 2003; Aug. 4, 2006
Detroit News, Feb. 17, 2004
New York Newsday, Dec. 5, 2004, p.C19
New York Times, Mar. 3, 2002
People, Nov. 22, 2004, p.123

Online Databases

Biography Resource Center Online, 2007, article from *Contemporary Black Biography,* 2006

Online Articles

http://sitemaker.umich.edu/livingmusic/home
(*Living Music* interview with Aaron Dworkin, Oct. 21, 2005)
http://www.macfound.org/site/c.lkLXJ8MQKrH/b.1038727/apps/s/content.asp?ct=1470799
(MacArthur Foundation, "Aaron Dworkin," no date)
http://www.metrotimes.com/editorial/story.asp?id=4626
(*Metro Times,* "Mystery of the Sphinx," Feb. 26, 2003)
http://www.umich.edu/news/MT/06/Spring06/story.html?MusicalGenius
(*Michigan Today,* "Musical Genius," Spring 2006)

ADDRESS

Aaron Dworkin
Sphinx Organization
400 Renaissance Center, Suite 2550
Detroit, MI 48243
Email info@sphinxmusic.org

WORLD WIDE WEB SITE

http://www.sphinxmusic.org

Will Ferrell 1967-

American Actor
Star of the Hit Films *Old School, Elf, Anchorman,* and *Talladega Nights*

BIRTH

John William Ferrell was born on July 16, 1967, in Irvine, California. Irvine, 40 miles south of Los Angeles, is one of the larger cities in densely populated Orange County. Will's father, Lee Ferrell, is a professional musician who worked for years with a rock group called the Righteous Brothers. His mother has served as a professor and administrator at Santa Ana Community College. He has one younger brother, Patrick.

YOUTH

Some comedians draw upon their difficult childhoods for comic material. Ferrell remembers his own childhood fondly. He was happy living in Irvine, he got along well with his brother and both of his parents, and he was popular in school. In an interview, Ferrell's mother described him as "very even tempered, very easygoing. His father and I kinda went, 'How'd he get like that?' You know those little Matchbox cars? Will would line up his Matchbox cars, by himself, and be totally happy. You'd say, 'You wanna go to Disneyland today or line up your cars?' And he'd have to think about it."

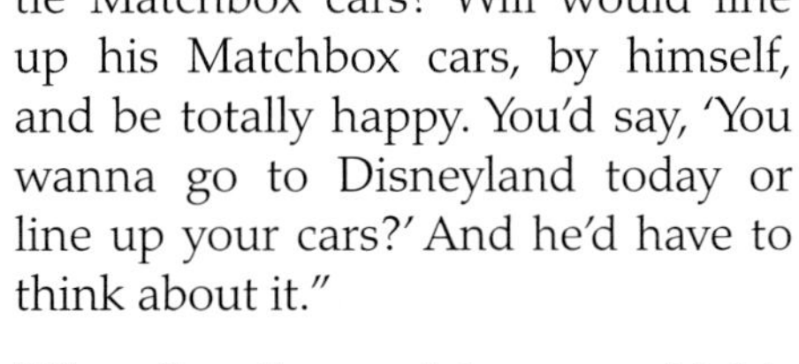

Ferrell's mother described him as "very even tempered, very easygoing. His father and I kinda went, 'How'd he get like that?' You know those little Matchbox cars? Will would line up his Matchbox cars, by himself, and be totally happy. You'd say, 'You wanna go to Disneyland today or line up your cars?' And he'd have to think about it."

When Ferrell was eight years old, his parents divorced. Even this setback had little effect on Ferrell's sunny personality. "I was the type of kid who would say, 'Hey! Look at the bright side! We'll have two Christmases,'" he recalled. His parents came through the divorce with no hostility and animosity and with a commitment to their children. The biggest difficulty stemmed from Lee Ferrell's line of work. As an entertainer, he had to go on the road with the Righteous Brothers for months at a time. He could not establish a successful solo career. He always struggled to make enough money to support his family. The son of a struggling musician, Will Ferrell grew up determined *not* to go into show business. Will wanted a stable, stay-at-home sort of job. He wanted to go into business.

EARLY MEMORIES

Ferrell has called third grade "a pivotal year" for him. He learned that he could make his classmates laugh if he pretended to smash his head against the wall, or if he tripped and fell on purpose. "That was a great way to make friends," he later said. At the same time, Ferrell realized that overdoing his comedy might get him in trouble with his teachers. He learned to be serious when necessary and to clown when possible—when it would not disrupt the classroom. "I wasn't obnoxious," he said. "I never got kicked out of class. I knew when enough was enough."

As he progressed through grade school and into high school, Ferrell grew tall and athletic. Standing six-foot-three by his late teens, he played basketball, soccer, and football. He was sometimes joined on teams by his brother, who grew to be six-foot-five. But the urge to make people laugh never left him. As a high school prank he formed a reptile club, even though he did not know anyone who owned a reptile. The club lasted for two meetings.

EDUCATION

Ferrell attended University High School in Irvine. He kept a busy schedule there, serving on the student council, becoming the team captain of his basketball squad, and serving as the kicker on the football team. All the while he earned good grades. He still knew how to get laughs without causing trouble, yet he never dreamed of a career in comedy. "I grew up around the entertainment industry and it took away all my illusions," he recalled. "I didn't want to do the same as my dad. I realized it was a month-to-month existence, with no real security."

Ferrell could not stop being funny, though. In his senior year of high school, he and a friend began making comedy skits out of the school's morning announcements and piping them through the intercom system. They did this with the full cooperation of the principal. Of course they had to write the material, and this proved to be another education for Ferrell in the art of comedy. He also did comic skits in school talent shows. When he graduated from University High, his classmates named him "Best Personality."

In 1986 Ferrell entered the University of Southern California, one of the state's largest colleges. He decided to major in sports information, leading to a career in public relations or broadcasting. This seemed like a safe and sensible plan. At the same time, he did not lose his sense of humor. As he progressed through college his pranks grew bolder. One of his favorites was dressing in a janitor's uniform and strolling into his friends' classes. He also engaged in "streaking"—running naked in public places, usually with a small group of his fraternity brothers from Delta Tau Delta.

Ferrell was not a top student academically at the University of Southern California, but he was easygoing and good looking. He earned an internship at a local television station in the sports department. To his great disappointment, he found he did not like the work. The only aspect of the job that appealed to him was the opportunity to appear on the air. "Midway through my training I realized I enjoyed performing for the camera much more than I enjoyed reporting," he said. Farrell graduated from USC in 1990 with a bachelor's degree in sports broadcasting, but his internship convinced him not to seek employment as a sportscaster.

FIRST JOBS

Uncertain about the direction he should take in life, Ferrell moved back in with his mother. He passed through a series of jobs and hated them all. He worked as a hotel valet, moving guests' cars to a parking garage. On his second day at work he tore a baggage rack off the top of a van by trying to drive it under a low-lying beam. A worse fate awaited him at another position — as a teller at the Wells Fargo Bank. After his first day on the job he was short $300. The following day he was short $280. He did not steal the money — he was just careless and error-prone as he served customers.

Ferrell's mother recognized his frustration with this series of unfulfilling jobs. She encouraged him to try his hand at comedy, even if he was worried about being able to make a living in the field. In 1991 he took her advice. He moved to Los Angeles, found an apartment, and auditioned for an improvisational group called The Groundlings.

CAREER HIGHLIGHTS

Early Comedy Work with The Groundlings

The Groundlings is a Los Angeles *improv* group composed of paid professionals and tuition-paying students at various levels of talent and experience. The word *improv* is short for "improvisational." In improv comedy, individual performers are given a situation or character and then expected to create comic dilemmas onstage without any rehearsal or written script. This spontaneous form of comedy requires quick thinking and a wide range of talent. The Groundlings offered classes for beginners, as well as advanced opportunities for actors and comedians who passed an audition. Ferrell passed the audition and began working with the advanced classes.

Before joining The Groundlings, Ferrell tried standup comedy, the type of comedy performed in front of an audience using a microphone. He had no success and decided that he was unsuited for standup. He has never really seen himself as a funny person: he could not draw upon an unusual appearance or a dark past for comic material. Improv offered a solution. It allowed Ferrell to *inhabit a character,* someone other than himself, and to act in ways that fit the character.

Ferrell discovered that he liked to do impressions of famous people. One of the first was baseball radio announcer Harry Caray. Now deceased and enshrined in the Baseball Hall of Fame, Caray was quite famous for his unique on-air style. Ferrell began to mimic his voice patterns and unbridled enthusiasm. Then he put his "Harry Caray" character into odd situations, such as auditioning for a play. This material worked well when Ferrell performed it at The Groundlings classes.

"I grew up around the entertainment industry and it took away all my illusions," Farrell recalled. "I didn't want to do the same as my dad. I realized it was a month-to-month existence, with no real security."

Ferrell also began to create original characters. With fellow Groundlings member Chris Kattan he began an ongoing routine about the fictitious Butabi brothers, a pair of losers who go out to dance clubs to try to meet women, only to be rejected time after time.

During the three years when he was learning improv, Ferrell needed part-time work in order to pay his bills. A friend of his, Viveca Paulin, helped him land a job at the auction house where she worked. The job gave Ferrell enough flexibility to attend auditions and to rehearse with The Groundlings. Gradually he began to get more and more paid work as an actor. He made guest appearances on television situation comedies like "Grace under Fire" and "Living Single," as well as commercials and low-budget comedy films, including *Bucket of Blood.* Even so he had to serve as a mall Santa Claus one winter. Little by little, however, Ferrell made progress. In 1994 he won a spot with The Groundlings' top professional group. Important show business executives came to watch his work, eventually leading to his move to "Saturday Night Live."

Auditioning for "Saturday Night Live"

"Saturday Night Live" began its run on late-night television in October 1975. More than 30 years later the show is still on the air, with a weekly live show featuring sketch comedy appearing late on Saturday nights. Its

Ferrell first found success on "SNL," particularly with his impressions of George W. Bush. In this mock presidential debate shortly before the 2000 election, Ferrell plays Bush and Darrell Hammond plays Vice President Al Gore.

edgy brand of rehearsed but spontaneous-looking comic skits has launched the film and TV careers of dozens of actors and actresses, including Dan Ackroyd, John Belushi, Chevy Chase, Billy Crystal, Jane Curtin, Tina Fey, Eddie Murphy, Bill Murray, Mike Myers, Chris Rock, Adam Sandler, and Molly Shannon. Each show includes short comedy sketches performed by cast members alongside the week's host, with musical numbers by a featured performer, usually one of the hottest acts around.

Just as "Saturday Night Live" has served as a proving ground for future movie stars, The Groundlings has served as a proving ground for "Saturday Night Live." Ferrell had been in The Groundlings' top performance group for only 10 months when a producer for "Saturday Night Live" came to see a performance. At that point "SNL" had fallen in popularity, and its production staff was eager to sign some new talent for the 1995 season. On the basis of his performance, Ferrell was invited to New York City to audition for "SNL" in front of its main producer, Lorne Michaels. Two fellow performers at The Groundlings, Chris Kattan and Cheri Oteri, were also asked to audition.

Onstage before Michaels, Ferrell launched into some of his best routines, including his take on Harry Caray and a one-man sketch in which a macho middle-class man becomes unhinged while simultaneously barbecuing meat and arguing with his children. Michaels invited Ferrell back for a business meeting to discuss adding him to the show. Ferrell did not quite know how to approach this meeting. He wondered if he should bring a comic twist to it, or simply play it straight. Finally he decided to stuff a briefcase with fake money and to pretend that *he* was trying to hire Lorne Michaels. The meeting turned out to be very serious, strictly business, and Ferrell never opened his briefcase. Then he was told to return for another meeting. Again he brought the briefcase, and again it stayed closed. When Michaels asked Ferrell to join the cast of "Saturday Night Live," the two men sealed the deal with a handshake. The unused briefcase full of fake cash became a memento that Ferrell has saved.

Becoming a Star on "SNL"

Ferrell started on "Saturday Night Live" in 1995. Just before he went on the air in his first appearance, he expressed some anxiety. "I never got a sense of why they picked me," he admitted. "I'm either very talented or they're in trouble." While he didn't have a strong first season, he soon became an audience favorite. He and Kattan performed some of their Groundlings material, including their Butabi brothers routine. And as the writers for the show began to notice Ferrell's ability to mimic famous people, they started writing sketches especially for him. He often lampooned such national figures as former Attorney General Janet Reno, "Jeopardy" host Alex Trebec, and singer Robert Goulet.

Ferrell came into his own, however, when he began to impersonate George W. Bush. The comedian first appeared as Bush even before Bush became president in 2000. After the election, he regularly spoofed President Bush. Ferrell managed to mimic Bush's mannerisms and speech patterns even though the comedian looked nothing like the president. Ferrell also offered a level of satire that clearly criticized the president's ability to run the country. As Marc Peyser wrote in *Newsweek,* "Ferrell hasn't been shy about criticizing his alter ego."

Ratings for "Saturday Night Live" improved during the seven seasons that Ferrell appeared on the show. Despite his early anxiety about whether he had enough talent for "SNL," he was nominated for an Emmy Award in 2001. Lorne Michaels even declared that Ferrell was "the center pillar" on the show for much of his seven-year run.

Starting a Film Career

Despite this success with "Saturday Night Live," Ferrell worried that he might not be able to advance his career beyond television if he stayed on the show for too long. So while continuing to appear on "SNL," he took small roles in movies when it wasn't taping. He appeared in *Austin Powers: International Man of Mystery* (1997), a parody of 1960s spy movies, especially the James Bond series. Mike Myers starred as the super-spy Austin Powers, and Ferrell appeared in a small role as Mustafa, one of Dr. Evil's henchmen. He reprised his role as Mustafa in the follow-up film, *Austin Powers: The Spy Who Shagged Me* (1999).

Ferrell's first starring role came in *A Night at the Roxbury* (1998), in which he co-starred with Chris Kattan, with whom he also wrote the script. The movie was based on the characters Steve and Doug Butabi, which they had first created for The Groundlings and then continued to develop on "Saturday Night Live." Steve and Doug Butabi are pathetic but lovable brothers. During the day they work at their father's fake plant store; at night they prowl music clubs, dressed in their matching polyester suits, bobbing their heads together in time to the music, and trying to meet women. Reviews of the movie were mixed, as many felt that what worked as short sketch was a bit belabored as a full-length movie.

"I'm at play every time I get to act," Ferrell once said. "That never leaves me. It comes through more in the characters with eternal optimism. Whether it's joy, or cockiness, it's fun to play attitude to the nth degree."

Ferrell had small parts in several additional movies while continuing to appear on "Saturday Night Live." In *Superstar* (1999), also based on an "SNL" skit, Molly Shannon starred as a nerdy Catholic schoolgirl, Mary Katherine Gallagher, who dreams of being famous. Ferrell played Sky Corrigan, on whom she has a crush. In *Dick* (1999), Ferrell played renowned journalist Bob Woodward. He and fellow *Washington Post* reporter Carl Bernstein were pivotal in uncovering the Watergate scandal that became the downfall of President Richard Nixon. But *Dick* provides a fairly silly version of this serious historical event. It centers around two teen girls, played by Michelle Williams and Kirsten Dunst, who become embroiled in the scandal. In *Zoolander* (2001), a send up of the modeling world starring Ben Stiller and Owen Wilson as vacuous male models,

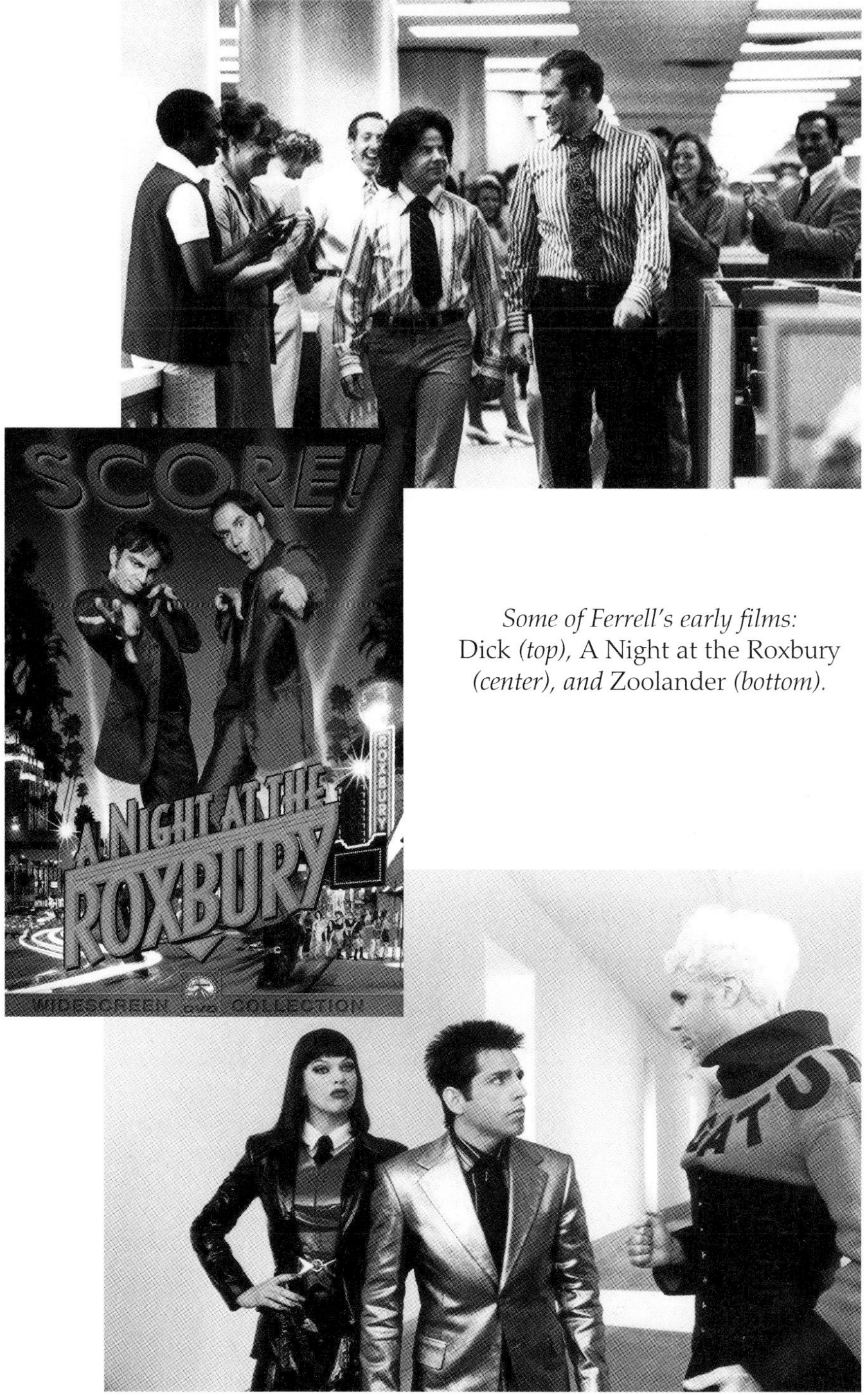

Some of Ferrell's early films:
Dick *(top),* A Night at the Roxbury *(center), and* Zoolander *(bottom).*

Two of the movies that made Ferrell a star: Old School *(top) and* Elf *(right).*

Ferrell played the evil fashion mogul Jacobim Mugatu, who plans to assassinate the prime minister of Malaysia to ensure cheap labor for the fashion industry.

Old School and *Elf*

In 2002, after seven seasons on "Saturday Night Live," Ferrell announced that he would retire from the show so he could spend more time making movies. That proved to be a turning point in his career, as he went on to appear in his second starring vehicle, *Old School* (2003). This comedy features Ferrell, Vince Vaughn, and Luke Wilson as a trio of aging men who decide to return to their glory days as college fraternity brothers. Ferrell is "Frank the Tank," the leader and most outrageous member of the gang. In one scene he convinces his friends to streak down a street and winds up sprinting naked all on his own—the other two chicken out.

Old School quickly became an audience favorite. Ferrell's many fans loved the film's raucous humor, as explained by David Denby. "It's party time, and the movie is wild and crude without being mean—it's a comedy of infantile regression, *Animal House* for grownups," Denby wrote. "The humor is hit or miss, but each of the three men is funny in his own way. Will Ferrell, of 'Saturday Night Live,' has a roly-poly childishness that reaches full flower in a sequence devoted to college athletics in which he waves a long red ribbon in graceful circles and assumes a crouching pose of artistic Olympian virtue." Reaction to the movie from critics was mixed, however, as in this comment by Robert Abele in a review of the movie for the *Los Angeles Times.* Abele wrote that Ferrell "expertly mines the humor in a man slipping backward down the evolutionary scale."

> *"It's party time, and the movie* [Old School] *is wild and crude without being mean—it's a comedy of infantile regression,* Animal House *for grownups," wrote reviewer David Denby. "[Ferrell] has a roly-poly childishness that reaches full flower in a sequence devoted to college athletics in which he waves a long red ribbon in graceful circles and assumes a crouching pose of artistic Olympian virtue."*

In Ferrell's next film, *Elf* (2003), he stars as Buddy, who was a baby when he crawled into Santa's bag one Christmas Eve and then was raised at the North Pole by Santa Claus (Ed Asner) and the elves. Like the elves and animated talking animals in his world, Buddy is happy and completely obsessed with Christmas. He knows he is different from the other elves, though. He towers over his friends and adopted father, and he cannot work as quickly as the other toymakers. When Buddy's North Pole father tells him he is adopted, Buddy decides to set out for New York City to find his real dad. Dressed in his outlandish elf clothing, brimming with high spirits, Buddy walks into

Manhattan and into the life of his biological father (James Caan) and his skeptical 10-year-old half-brother. Faced with the cynicism of his family and other New Yorkers, he becomes determined to restore the true meaning of Christmas.

Ferrell liked the *Elf* script because it allowed him to clown, but also to show a range of endearing emotions. "I'm at play every time I get to act," he once said. "That never leaves me. It comes through more in the characters with eternal optimism. Whether it's joy, or cockiness, it's fun to play attitude to the nth degree." The film's director, Jon Favreau, had a slightly different take on his approach to acting. "His humor has a real vulnerability to it," said Favreau. "He was really sweet and nice and quiet. It was hard to evaluate his energy on that set, though, because he was always naked."

"
*"*Anchorman *is slyer than most other dumb comedies out there without ever making the mistake of taking itself too seriously," said Leah Rozen. "How could it when its hero, talking himself up to a prospective date, announces in his most sepulchral tone, 'I'm very important. I have many leather-bound books.' It's this kind of goofy line, and scene, that makes* Anchorman *a breezy hoot."*
"

Elf proved to be a big hit with critics, as in this comment from Lisa Schwarzbaum. "The disarming comedic tone—silly and novel in its lack of cynicism—is driven by the fearless, cheerful unself-consciousness of Will Ferrell, a big man last seen streaking (all too unself-consciously) through *Old School*. Now wearing lime green polar couture and a humiliation-proof grin, he's a sight for dour eyes." Audiences loved the movie as well. *Elf* grossed $31 million at the box office the weekend it opened in November of 2003. Since then it has earned more than $175 million in theaters and DVD rentals. *Old School* enjoyed similar financial success. Made for $24 million, it has earned more than $145 million and has become a huge hit on DVD. The combination of these two totals crowned Ferrell as "the comic lead that everyone in Hollywood wants to cast," explained analyst Sharon Waxman. Despite all this success, Ferrell still felt uneasy about his chosen career. "I always think of alternative careers, in case this thing doesn't work out," he said in 2004—after *Old School* and *Elf* had established him as a star.

Ferrell as the title character Ron Burgundy in Anchorman.

Anchorman and *Talladega Nights*

Ferrell's next big success came in the movie *Anchorman: The Legend of Ron Burgundy* (2004). Long before he scored the dual successes of *Old School* and *Elf,* Ferrell had been co-writing a screenplay with Adam McKay, a co-worker from "Saturday Night Live." That movie, *Anchorman,* pokes fun at the macho, all-male realm of television broadcasting in the 1970s. Ferrell appears as the title character, Ron Burgundy, a sexist anchorman in San Diego who believes that all women adore him and that women don't belong in the newsroom. He has to deal with this prejudice when a pretty, ambitious young woman (Christina Applegate) lands a position at his TV station.

Anchorman found favor with a variety of audiences and performed well at the box office, with reviewers pointing to Ferrell's performance. "[Ferrell] does a variation on his specialty—the completely unjustified egomaniac," wrote Owen Gleiberman. "Ron is a homegrown Austin Powers. He's blind entitlement wrapped around a core of utter dimness." Leah Rozen had this praise for the movie. "With little on its mind besides poking fun at egotistical TV-news Twinkies, *Anchorman* is slyer than most other dumb comedies out there without ever making the mistake of taking itself too seriously. How could it when its hero, talking himself up to a prospective date, announces in his most sepulchral tone, 'I'm very important. I have many leather-bound books.' It's this kind of goofy line, and scene, that makes *Anchorman* a breezy hoot."

Ferrell appeared in several films in 2005. He starred in the serious Woody Allen movie *Melinda and Melinda* and the family comedy *Kicking and Screaming,* a satire about the competitive nature of amateur soccer coaches in pee wee leagues. *Kicking and Screaming* features Ferrell as a coach with a grudge against his father, played by veteran actor Robert Duvall. As part of their feud, the two characters coach rival teams, using every trick to win games against one another. Although the film did not perform as well as *Elf, Kicking and Screaming* found its supporters. *Chicago Tribune* columnist Robert K. Elder called Ferrell "a mow-you-down comic engine" in his review of the movie.

“

"Ricky Bobby is at once a creature of pure, extravagant absurdity and a curiously vulnerable, sympathetic figure," wrote reviewer A. O. Scott. "This movie is the real thing."

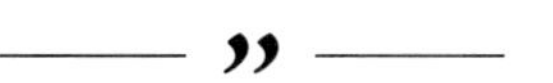

Also in 2005 Ferrell appeared in *Bewitched* with Nicole Kidman. Based on a 1960s-era television show, *Bewitched* tells the story of a down-and-out actor (Ferrell) who attempts to revive his career by appearing in a movie version of the TV show. His co-star (Kidman) proves to have true magical powers, helping them both to shine—and to fall in love. Topping off a busy year, Ferrell took the role of the hapless Nazi playwright Franz Liebkind in the movie version of the Broadway musical *The Producers.* Somehow, in addition to all those major features, he managed to offer his voice to the animated comedy *Curious George* and to complete cameo roles in *Starsky & Hutch* and *The Wedding Crashers.*

Ferrell again teamed with Adam McKay to write the 2006 hit *Talladega Nights: The Ricky Bobby Story.* McKay also directed the film. *Talladega Nights* satirizes one of America's favorite sports—NASCAR racing. It lampoons the sport's constant use of product advertising and its egotistical stars, all without offending its many fans. None too intelligent but brimming with personality, Ricky Bobby, as played by Ferrell, traces his addiction to speedy cars to his birth in the back of a souped-up Chevrolet. His father is a race car driver, so naturally Ricky follows his dad into the sport and becomes a huge success. But that success sometimes comes at the expense of his best friend, fellow driver Cal Naughton, Jr. (played by

Ferrell (right) and John C. Reilly (left) in Talladega Nights.

John C. Reilly). Hailing from North Carolina, Ricky sports a Southern accent and is devoted to his beautiful but cunning wife (Leslie Bibb). A rival driver from France named Jean Girard invades Ricky's ideal life and provides bitter competition. The Frenchman, performed by Sacha Baron Cohen, sips espresso and otherwise challenges the all-American macho image of NASCAR.

Talladega Nights was one of the most successful summer movies of 2006, becoming a hit with audiences and critics alike. "Ricky Bobby is at once a creature of pure, extravagant absurdity and a curiously vulnerable, sympathetic figure," wrote reviewer A. O. Scott. "This movie is the real thing." According to Kenneth Turan, "There is a real sincerity to Ferrell's characterization . . . an ability to take silly things so completely seriously that laughter inevitably results."

Current Projects

After a string of comedies, Ferrell appeared in a more serious movie late in 2006. In *Stranger than Fiction,* he played Harold Crick, a dull Internal Revenue Service agent who suddenly hears a women's voice in his head narrating the details of his life. Crick discovers that he has become the main character in a novel and that the author of the novel plans to end the book with his death. Desperate to save himself, Crick launches a search for the author, played by Emma Thompson. Ferrell said of the film,

Ferrell in a scene from Stranger than Fiction.

"I think it's the best thing I've done, with some amazing actors. Forget about me, it's really an amazing film just by itself."

Next up for Ferrell is *Blades of Glory*, which is due for release in early 2007. It's a comedy about the first male figure-skating pair, played by Ferrell and Jon Heder (from *Napoleon Dynamite*). They're opposed in the Olympics by another duo, played by Amy Poehler and Will Arnett. The idea of a male figure-skating pair creates some funny possibilities, particularly the skating routines. "When those guys lifted their legs, it was a beautiful move," said Poehler. "But they had some chafing problems." *People* magazine described it as "Think *Chariots of Fire* meets the Ice Capades meets *Talladega Nights*, and you've got *Blades of Glory*."

MARRIAGE AND FAMILY

Ferrell married his longtime friend Viveca Paulin in August 2000. They have two sons: Magnus, who was born in March 2004, and Mattias, who was born in December 2006. Ferrell and his family live in Los Angeles. When he is working on location outside California, his wife and sons travel with him as often as they can.

HOBBIES AND OTHER INTERESTS

Ferrell's busy work schedule leaves him little time to indulge in hobbies. He acts, writes, and serves as an executive producer on his major films.

Nevertheless, he has found an outside interest—distance running. He and his wife both compete occasionally in marathons. In 2003 he was featured on the cover of *Runner's World* magazine. Ferrell sees his interest in running as a natural outcome of his athletic youth. "If anything," he said, "it's given me more energy, more of a focus and drive in other areas of my life."

SELECTED TELEVISION AND MOVIE CREDITS

"Saturday Night Live," 1995-2002
Bucket of Blood, 1995
Austin Powers: International Man of Mystery, 1997
Men Seeking Women, 1997
A Night at the Roxbury, 1998 (co-writer, with Chris Kattan)
Superstar, 1999
Dick, 1999
The Suburbans, 1999
Austin Powers: The Spy Who Shagged Me, 1999
Drowning Mona, 2000
The Ladies Man, 2000
"The Oblongs," 2001
Zoolander, 2001
Jay and Silent Bob Strike Back, 2001
Old School, 2003
Elf, 2003
Starsky & Hutch, 2004
Anchorman: The Legend of Ron Burgundy, 2004 (co-writer, with Adam McKay)
Melinda and Melinda, 2005
Kicking and Screaming, 2005
Bewitched, 2005
The Producers, 2005
Curious George, 2005 (voice for animation)
The Wedding Crashers, 2005
Talladega Nights: The Ricky Bobby Story, 2006 (co-writer, with Adam McKay)
Stranger than Fiction, 2006

FURTHER READING

Books

Epstein, Dwayne. *Will Ferrell,* 2005 (juvenile)
Miller, James A., and Tom Shales. *Live From New York: An Uncensored History of Saturday Night Live, as Told By Its Stars, Writers, and Guests,* 2003

Periodicals

Chicago Tribune, Oct. 5, 2006, p.C1
Current Biography Yearbook, 2003
Esquire, Dec. 2003, p.162
GQ, Dec. 2006, p.296
Los Angeles Times, May 7, 2002, Calendar, p.1
New York Times, Jan. 25, 2001, p. E1; May 9, 2004, p.A2; Aug. 4, 2006, p.E1
Newsweek, Feb. 19, 2001, p.56; July 12, 2004, p.58
People, Apr. 6, 1998, p.143; Nov. 24, 2003, p.71; Nov. 20, 2006, p.83
Time, Nov. 10, 2003, p.90
Variety, Oct. 5, 1998, p.68

Online Databases

Biography Resource Center Online, 2007

ADDRESS

Will Ferrell
Creative Artists Agency
9830 Wilshire Blvd.
Beverly Hills, CA 90212

WORLD WIDE WEB SITES

http://www.nbc.com/Saturday_Night_Live/bios/Will_Ferrell.shtml
http://www.oldschool-themovie.com
http://www.elfmovie.com
http://www.anchorman-themovie.com
http://www.sonypictures.com/movies/talladeganights

Sarah Blaffer Hrdy 1946-

American Anthropologist and Primatologist
Pioneer in the Scientific Study of Motherhood

BIRTH

Sarah Blaffer Hrdy (rhymes with "birdie") was born on July 11, 1946, in Dallas, Texas. Her parents were both members of prominent Texas families. Her father, John H. Blaffer, was heir to an oil fortune, while her mother, Camilla Davis, came from a Dallas banking family. Sarah was the third of four daughters born to the Blaffers before they had their fifth and last child, a son.

YOUTH

Sarah Blaffer grew up in an atmosphere of privilege. Her parents were wealthy enough to afford a nanny for their large family, and their children were able to attend the best private schools. Still, it was an era in which many experts believed that children should not be coddled. "My mother's idea of good management was that if a child became too attached to a nanny, it was time to hire a new one, lest maternal control be diminished," Hrdy recalled. "This meant I was reared by a succession of governesses." Still, she added, "No one ever doubted that my mother loved her five children."

"My mother's idea of good management was that if a child became too attached to a nanny, it was time to hire a new one, lest maternal control be diminished," Hrdy recalled. "This meant I was reared by a succession of governesses."

Hrdy also credits her mother with supporting her intellectual curiosity and deep love of learning. This encouragement may have stemmed in part from her mother's own youthful experiences. Camilla Davis had graduated from college with the hope of attending law school. Instead, she had returned to Dallas society and married, as her family expected. Young Sarah grew up in this same "high society" environment, one in which a young woman's debut at a society ball was widely regarded as one of the most important moments in her life. Sarah, however, was more concerned with intellectual pursuits, and "in the social environment in which I grew up, that was not acceptable," she recalled.

As the third-oldest sister, however, Sarah enjoyed a greater level of freedom than her older sisters. "I was the heiress to spare, and that left me a lot of freedom," she said. When at 16 she was given the chance to attend an academically challenging boarding school, she enrolled with her mother's blessing.

EDUCATION

After graduating from high school in the early 1960s, Hrdy entered her mother's old school, Wellesley College. She transferred to Radcliffe College, formerly the women's college of Harvard University, when Harvard was segregated by sex. Hrdy graduated summa cum laude ("with highest honors") with a bachelor's degree in 1969. Her senior thesis, on the Mayan myth of the bat demon, was published in 1972 as *The Black-Man of Zinacantan: A Central American Legend.* That same year she married Daniel B. Hrdy, a fellow student at Harvard.

Hrdy then briefly studied filmmaking at Stanford University in hopes of making educational films for people in underdeveloped countries. She lost interest, though, when it became clear that her film classes were primarily concerned with Hollywood and popular moviemaking. Around this same time, a biology seminar at Stanford inspired her to pursue a doctorate in anthropology, the scientific study of human origins and behavior. She returned to Harvard University and earned her doctoral degree or doctorate (PhD) in anthropology in 1975.

CAREER HIGHLIGHTS

Pioneering Observations of Langurs

Earning a doctoral degree, or PhD, usually includes doing significant intellectual research and then writing it up in a book length paper called a dissertation. For her doctoral research, Hrdy decided to study the Hanuman langur monkeys of Mount Abu in Rajasthan, India. Hanuman langurs are sacred to local residents, who feed them and protect them

Hrdy watching langur monkeys in India.

from harm whenever possible. But many observers believed that these attitudes were contributing to the species' increasing problems with overpopulation in the region. Hrdy's decision to study the Hanuman langur monkeys also stemmed in part from reports that male langurs in the region were killing infant monkeys. Some scholars speculated that this troubling behavior was a reaction to the increasingly overcrowded conditions in the monkeys' territory.

Hrdy spent almost 1,500 hours between 1971 and 1975 observing Hanuman langurs in their natural environment. She documented that under normal conditions, adult male langurs seemed very tolerant of infants. But she discovered that when a new male took over leadership of a langur tribe, he would attack infants sired by other males. Hrdy realized that although the practice of "infanticide" (baby-killing) by the Hanuman langur males was shocking, there was actually a biological motive behind it: without a baby to nurse, females would be ready to mate sooner, ensuring the new "alpha" (dominant) male could produce more of his own offspring.

Hrdy detailed her observations and conclusions in her 1977 book *The Langurs of Abu: Female and Male Strategies of Reproduction.* In addition to explaining the reasons for male infanticide, she noted that langur females had their own methods for dealing with this behavior. When a new alpha male came into the tribe, females with infants would pretend to be fertile and have sex with the male. He would then believe that any new babies might be his, and leave them alone.

When Hrdy first published her study, many fellow scientists dismissed her conclusions. They suggested that the monkeys she studied were abnormal or that she had used flawed methods of observation. In the decades since she first proposed her theories about infanticide, however, scientists have observed similar behavior in a wide range of species including mice, wasps, fish, foxes, deer, bears, and lions, as well as several other species of monkeys.

Challenging Conventional Wisdom

Despite the controversial nature of her thesis work, Hrdy's academic career soared. After completing her PhD, she worked as a lecturer in biological anthropology at Harvard from 1975 to 1976, and then earned a postdoctoral fellowship in Harvard's biology department from 1977 to 1978. She continued doing field research on the Mount Abu langurs until 1979, when the tense political climate in the region and the needs of her toddler daughter, born in 1977, convinced her to stop. "Field work is incompatible with having children," she noted. "You compromise to have a family, but you don't give everything up."

Hrdy became an associate in biological anthropology at Harvard's Peabody Museum in 1979. She also spent time teaching at the American Institute of Indian Studies in New Delhi, India, and at Rice University in Houston, Texas. Throughout this period, Hrdy found that working in a male-dominated field of research carried special challenges for a woman. Some fellow scholars dismissed her research and conclusions simply because of her gender. "I was blown away," she remembered. "All my life I had felt guilty for being overprivileged, and all of a sudden people were discriminating against *me.*"

Undaunted by this hostility, Hrdy pressed on with her research. "It was painful at the time, but I think it was probably very fruitful," she admitted. "I started to challenge conventional wisdom, which is a good thing to do." She turned from studying infanticide to exploring the female role in mating practices. The result was her 1981 work *The Woman That Never Evolved,* which the *New York Times Book Review* named a Notable Book of the Year in Science and Social Science.

"All my life I had felt guilty for being over-privileged, and all of a sudden people were discriminating against me," remembered Hrdy.

In *The Woman That Never Evolved,* Hrdy challenged the idea put forth by Charles Darwin, pioneer of evolutionary theory, that females play a passive role in sexual selection of mates. The 19th-century culture in which Darwin lived had always thought of women as faithful creatures who were uninterested in sex, but Hrdy wanted to test this belief. By studying primates (humans and their closest relatives, apes and monkeys), she hoped to discover "why some current notions of what it means to be female depict natures that never did, and never could have, evolved within the primate lineage."

Hrdy's book detailed many different patterns of behavior in primate females. She pointed out that some have one mate for life, while others take many mates; some have limited breeding seasons, while others can breed throughout the year; some display signs of being fertile, while others do not; some only have sex when fertile, while others have sex at other times. By exploring the many variations in female primate behavior, Hrdy "clearly demonstrates that there cannot be any generally ordained role for

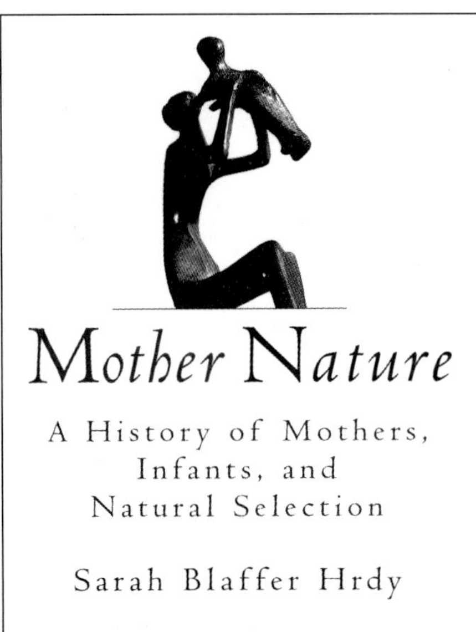

In her book Mother Nature, *Hrdy uses her research into primate behavior to explore the bond between human mothers and their babies.*

females," Paul A. Colinvaux noted in the *New York Times.* The book was also warmly received by feminist activists who hailed it for pointing out the complexity of female sexuality. For her part, Hrdy called her work "an effort to expand the range of attributes encompassed by a term like *female nature.* . . . Rather than reducing female nature to any single set of stereotypes, we talk about a whole range of possibilities."

Exploring the Nature of Motherhood

Hrdy was gratified by the response to her work and the greater acceptance that her theories were receiving. At the same time, though, she noted that "I found myself torn between my work and an admittedly adorable but insatiably demanding human baby." When a dismissive colleague told her to "devote more time and study and thought to raising a healthy daughter," the remark hit upon a secret guilt—but it also inspired her to think about the nature of motherhood. Were all mothers really the selfless, giving creatures of popular myth? Hrdy decided to explore the subject, "to understand not just who I am, but how creatures like me came to be."

In 1984 Hrdy took a post as professor of anthropology at the University of California, Davis, where she increasingly focused her research on the subject of motherhood. In 1987 she received a Guggenheim fellowship, a prestigious financial grant, to write a book on the subject. Nine years later she retired as professor emeritus from the University of California to focus more time on her project and her family. In all, she spent almost 15 years researching and writing *Mother Nature: A History of Mothers, Infants, and Natural Selection,* which was published in 1999.

In *Mother Nature,* Hrdy examined the numerous primate methods of mothering as well as the ways in which various human cultures throughout history have raised children. Again, she discovered there was no single strategy that was "natural" to mothers. Instead, their methods ranged "from total commitment to absence of caring," she stated. "The way any given mother responds will vary with her circumstances — how old she is, her physical condition, how much social support she can anticipate." For instance, in ancient Rome babies were often abandoned on roadsides. A similar phenomenon occurred in 18th-century Europe, where orphanages became badly overcrowded with thousands of children abandoned by impoverished parents. Hrdy further documented how concepts of parenthood vary in modern cultures. She noted, for instance, that some cultures place a higher value on one gender over another.

Hrdy's work emphasized that successfully raising a child requires enormous expenditures of time and effort from parents in general and mothers in particular. Given this reality, Hrdy suggests in *Mother Nature* that humans evolved as cooperative breeders. Mothers are "resourceful opportunists who elicit help from a range of different parties," Hrdy noted. These assistants, whom she calls "allomothers" (from the Greek "allo," meaning "other than"), can include the mother's mates, mother, brothers and sisters, and older children. Unrelated females from the same tribe can also help out.

> "
>
> *In her book* **Mother Nature,** *Hrdy wanted to explore "our preconceptions about women—yes, they're nurturing; yes, they're cooperative; but they're also competitive, destructive, ambitious and creative. The same goes for mothers."*
>
> "

Hrdy also asserted that women who are ambitious and career-oriented are in some ways actually well-equipped for motherhood; after all, successful, high-status females have more power and resources to spend on their children. It is only "because jobs, status and resource defense occur in separate domains from child-rearing" that women face a conflict between work and parenting, she explained. In *Mother Nature* she hopes to expand "our preconceptions about women — yes, they're nurturing; yes, they're cooperative; but they're also competitive, destructive, ambitious and creative. The same goes for mothers."

Mother Nature garnered a lot of attention when it was published. *Library Journal* and *Publishers Weekly* both named the book to their Best Books of 1999 lists, and it was a finalist for the PEN USA West Literary Award for Research Nonfiction in 2000. In 2001 Hrdy's peers in the American Anthropological Association awarded the book the Howells Prize for

Outstanding Contribution to Biological Anthropology. In the London *Independent,* Daniel Britten called *Mother Nature* "a splendidly thought-provoking book. . . . With one great stride Blaffer Hrdy has carried the debate about parenting to a higher stage of adaptation. It should be required reading for parents, feminists, and evolutionary scientists alike."

Acceptance and Respect

Scientists need to go beyond simple data collection and theorize and imagine how things might work, Hrdy believes. "You're trying to model what might be true and to generate the hypotheses that you want to look at," she noted. "Then you have the actual collection of data and all the methodologies that go into that. Imaginary worlds have a place in science."

Hrdy's early struggles with her male colleagues have vanished. The quality of her research and insights into human behavior finally forced her peers to give her the respect and praise that she deserved. She was elected to the National Academy of Sciences and became a fellow of Animal Behavior Society in 1990. Two years later she was invited to become a fellow of the American Academy of Arts and Sciences. In addition, she has served on editorial boards for several scholarly journals in the fields of primatology, anthropology, and evolution.

During this same period, Hrdy became known for her efforts to make science understandable to general audiences. She created the 1988 episode "Monkeys of Abu" for the TV series "National Geographic Explorer" and consulted on the 1990 series "Human Nature" for the British Broadcasting Corporation (BBC) and the 2001 series "Evolution" for the Public Broadcasting System (PBS). She also is a regular contributor to such popular magazines as *Natural History.*

Hrdy's enthusiasm and curiosity about anthropology remains undiminished. In recent years she has devoted much of her efforts to the study of genetic inheritance patterns. She is also considering writing what she calls a "history of the human family." But Hrdy admits that she has great concerns about the health and vitality of human families of the future. "Now, women are conceiving when they don't have the kind of social supports needed for offspring," she said. "And [the offspring] are surviv-

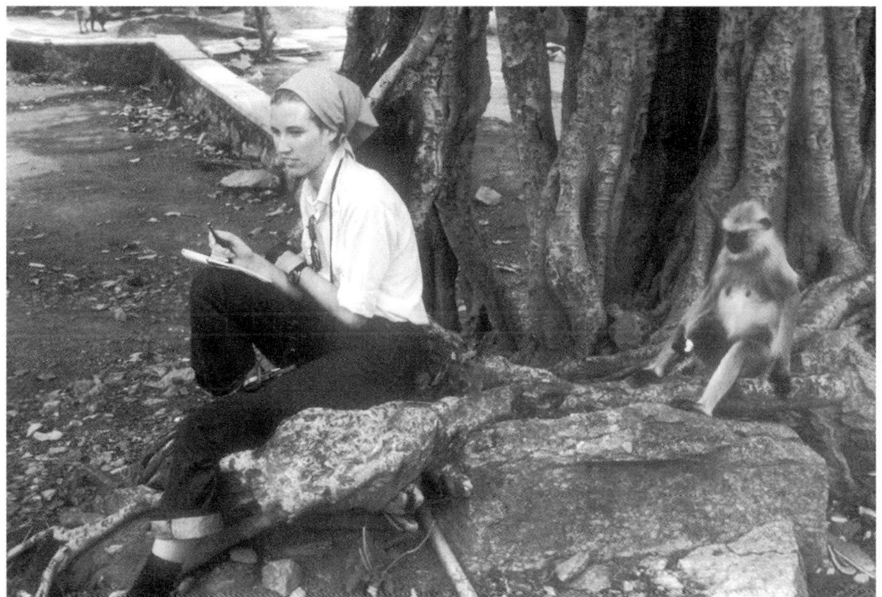

In this shot of Hrdy in India, it's unclear who is watching who.

ing in large numbers. This is new. . . . The creatures down the line may not be recognizably human. They may be smart, they may be bipedal, they may have language. But how nice are they going to be?"

Hrdy believes that thinking about such issues is vitally important to science. She asserts that scientists need to go beyond simple data collection and theorize and imagine how things might work: "You're trying to model what might be true and to generate the hypotheses that you want to look at," she noted. "Then you have the actual collection of data and all the methodologies that go into that. Imaginary worlds have a place in science."

MARRIAGE AND FAMILY

Sarah Blaffer met fellow student Daniel B. Hrdy in an undergraduate anthropology class at Harvard. She claims that she fell in love with the future physician and professor of infectious diseases "almost from the moment I first set eyes on him." In 1972 they married in Kathmandu, Nepal, during a break from their doctoral research. They have three children: Catherine (known as "Katrinka"), born in 1977; a second daughter, Sasha, born in 1982; and son Niko, born in 1986. The Hrdys live on a 1,000-acre walnut farm in Winters, California.

"

"Now, women are conceiving when they don't have the kind of social supports needed for offspring," Hrdy said. "And [the offspring] are surviving in large numbers. This is new. . . . The creatures down the line may not be recognizably human. They may be smart, they may be bipedal, they may have language. But how nice are they going to be?"

"

HOBBIES AND OTHER INTERESTS

Hrdy and her husband harvest almost 300 tons of walnuts every year on their farm. They allow flocks of wild turkeys to roam the farm, giving them and nearby students a chance to observe the birds' natural behavior. Hrdy also owns several Rhodesian Ridgebacks, a breed of large hunting dog with African origins. She enjoys listening to "books on tape" when she travels, especially works by such classic authors as George Eliot — the pseudonym of Mary Ann Evans, an early British feminist.

SELECTED WRITINGS

The Black-Man of Zinacantan: A Central American Legend, 1972
The Langurs of Abu: Female and Male Strategies of Reproduction, 1977
The Woman That Never Evolved, 1981
Infanticide: Comparative and Evolutionary Perspectives, 1984 (editor, with Glenn Hausfater)
Mother Nature: A History of Mothers, Infants and Natural Selection, 1999

HONORS AND AWARDS

Member, National Academy of Sciences: 1990
Fellow, Animal Behavior Society: 1990
Fellow, American Academy of Arts and Sciences: 1992
Howells Prize for Outstanding Contribution to Biological Anthropology (American Anthropological Association): 2001, for *Mother Nature: A History of Mothers, Infants and Natural Selection*

FURTHER READING

Books

Hrdy, Sarah Blaffer. *The Woman That Never Evolved,* 1981
Hrdy, Sarah Blaffer. *Mother Nature,* 1999

Periodicals

Current Biography Yearbook, 2000
Discover, Sep. 1996, p.72; Mar. 2003, p.40
Houston Chronicle, Oct. 31, 1999, Lifestyle p.3
Independent (London), Nov. 14, 1999, p.10
New Scientist, Mar. 24, 2003, p.46; Apr. 8, 2006, p.50
New York Times, Nov. 15, 1981, sec.7, p.9; Feb. 8, 2000, p.F1
Omni, June 1988, p.91
Radcliffe Quarterly, Summer 2000

Online Databases

Biography Resource Center Online, 2007, article from *Contemporary Authors Online,* 2004

ADDRESS

Sarah Blaffer Hrdy
Professor Emeritus
Department of Anthropology
212 Young Hall
University of California
Davis, CA 95616

WORLD WIDE WEB SITES

http://www.citrona.com

Keira Knightley 1985-

British Actress

Star of *Bend It Like Beckham, Pride and Prejudice,* and *Pirates of the Caribbean*

BIRTH

Kiera Christina Knightley (pronounced "KEE-ra") was born on March 26, 1985, in the southwest London suburb of Teddington, England. She later changed the spelling of her first name from Kiera to Keira to make it easier for international audiences to pronounce. She was the second child of

Will Knightley, a stage actor, and Sharman Macdonald, a playwright who once worked as an actress. Keira has one older brother, Caleb, who was born in 1979. He is also involved in the performing arts, having worked as a musician, sound engineer, and television studio manager.

Keira's birth was the result of a bet between her parents. Jobs in the theater were hard to find, and money was so tight that they were uncertain they could afford to have a second child. "My mum was desperate for another child, and my dad told her that the only way they could afford to have one was if she sold a play." Apparently his suggestion worked. In 1984 Macdonald's first play, *When I Was a Girl, I Used to Scream and Shout,* was staged in London. It won an Evening Standard Award and ran for eight years. Its success gave the couple the financial stability they needed to have a second child. Soon after its sale, Keira joined older brother Caleb.

YOUTH

Knightley was three years old the first time she asked her parents for an agent, even though she didn't know what an agent was. (An agent manages artists' careers by helping them find work.) She had heard her parents talking on the phone with their agents, so she wanted one of her own. Her parents refused. They wanted her to focus on her schoolwork, especially when they later discovered young Keira was having trouble learning to read. Although she was never formally diagnosed, she believes she had dyslexia, a learning disorder in which people have trouble recognizing and decoding words, which can make reading and spelling difficult. People with dyslexia often have trouble with reading comprehension. When Keira still wouldn't drop the idea of an agent, her mother made a bargain with her: if she would spend a summer reading for an hour every day, they would find her an agent. She fulfilled her end of the deal and got her first agent at the age of six.

Knightley's parents knew how difficult it could be to make a living as an actor and wanted to be sensible about their daughter's career. She was allowed to act only during school vacations, and only if she kept her grades up. Despite these restrictions, young Keira got her first job at age seven. She started out in a couple of commercials and earned some small television parts. Her first role was in a 1993 TV movie, *Royal Celebration,* billed as "Little Girl." She soon followed with a part in her first film, *A Village Affair* (1994). Knightley noted that these early roles had her "running into the picture saying 'Mummy' and 'Daddy' a lot and then running out of it again." She also earned roles as the younger version of adult characters in the films *Innocent Lies* (1995) and *Coming Home* (1998), and she played a princess in the TV movie *Treasure Seekers* (1996). Although she enjoyed acting, she had no idea what kind of success, if any, lay ahead of her.

EDUCATION

Knightley attended her local secondary school, Teddington School. Through hard work she overcame her reading difficulties and finished with top grades. She then was faced with a decision about what to do next. In England, compulsory secondary school ends at age 16. After that, some students leave school, but those who want further education can attend school for an additional two years before taking university entrance exams and then going on to university. This additional two years of schooling is referred to as "sixth form." Knightley began taking her sixth form at nearby Esher College, focusing on liberal arts such as art, history, and English literature. Because her acting career was taking off, however, she dropped out during her first year to work full-time; she also turned down a place at the London Academy of Music and Drama.

Knightley has often said she regrets not finishing college, but notes that "not having letters after my name won't define me as a person." She intends to pursue some kind of continuing education, explaining that "there's never an excuse to stop learning."

CAREER HIGHLIGHTS

Early Television and Film Roles

As a teenager Knightley began earning larger and more prominent parts. In 1998, she appeared in the TV miniseries of Charles Dickens's *Oliver Twist.* Her supporting role as Rose, a girl who assists the title character, was secondary but important. The miniseries was broadcast on both sides of the Atlantic, making it her first appearance on American television.

Her next role was in a film eagerly awaited by audiences all over the world: *Star Wars: Episode I—The Phantom Menace* (1999). Only sharp-eyed viewers noticed her in the film, though. She played Sabé, a servant who acts as a stand-in for Queen Amidala, played by actress Natalie Portman. When the two actresses were wearing their makeup, they looked so similar that their own mothers had trouble telling them apart. No wonder, then, that many viewers didn't notice Knightley and believed that Portman was playing both parts. Because the existence of Knightley's character Sabé as a decoy for Queen Amidala was a key plot twist, her part in the film wasn't publicized. She received little notice for the film, but it did give her valuable experience acting in a major Hollywood blockbuster.

At age 16 Knightley earned her first starring role, as the title character in the American TV movie *Princess of Thieves* (2001). Knightley trained for several weeks in archery, sword fighting, and horse riding for her role as Gwyn, the daughter of Robin Hood and Maid Marian. In the film her character disguises herself as a boy to battle her father's old enemy, the Sheriff of Nottingham. That same year Knightley also appeared in *The Hole,* a psychological thriller. She plays snobbish, shallow Frankie, one of four teenagers who hide in an underground bunker to avoid a school field trip. They get locked in and two weeks later, only one of the four emerges alive. While the film was only a modest success, it was a chance for the actress to take a more mature role.

Knightley continued to find more challenging roles in 2002. In the film *Pure,* she starred as a pregnant, teenaged heroin addict who has already had one child taken from her by social services. It was only a supporting role in a small, independent film, but it enabled her to demonstrate her acting range. In 2002 she also earned her first adult starring role in the TV miniseries of *Dr. Zhivago,* based on the classic novel by Boris Pasternak. The story is set in Russia during the early 20th century and focuses on the doomed romance between the title character and the beautiful nurse Lara. As Lara, Knightley had to portray the character from ages 16 to 32. The role was a major challenge, but the young actress was up to the task. Her passionate portrayal of Lara brought her to the attention of TV audiences in both Britain and the United States.

Even though Knightley had captained her school's soccer team, "I still had to learn to play for Beckham, because my version of playing soccer was being fast and kicking people in the shins."

”

Bend It Like Beckham

Knightley's first big success in motion pictures came in *Bend It Like Beckham* (2002). While still in school she had played a role in what was expected to be a small British movie about women's football (as soccer is called outside the U.S.). Knightley played Jules (short for Juliet), a British girl who is dedicated to her women's soccer team. Parminder Nagra played Jess, a girl of Indian descent who wants to play soccer, although her traditional parents push her to focus on school and marriage. Jules sees Jess messing around with a soccer ball and convinces her to join the local team. For both Jules and Jess, playing soccer means defying the

Bend It Like Beckham *(left) was the first film to bring Knightley widespread attention and success.*

Knightley with Orlando Bloom in Pirates of the Caribbean: The Curse of the Black Pearl *(below).*

wishes of their parents and dealing with the hard feelings that creates. The film's title, *Bend It Like Beckham,* refers to how British soccer superstar David Beckham can kick a ball so that it curves into the goal.

Preparing for the role required Knightley to train intensively for several weeks. Even though she had captained her school's soccer team, "I still had to learn to play for *Beckham,* because my version of playing soccer was being fast and kicking people in the shins." When the film debuted in Britain in spring 2002, it became a surprise success. In 2003 the movie was released in the U.S., where reaction to the movie was very strong, especially among young female athletes. The film earned a respectable $32.5 million in America. Much of its success was due to the chemistry between Knightley and Nagra, whose believable friendship was at the center of this coming-of-age story.

In Pirates, *Knightley was drawn to the feisty spirit of Elizabeth Swann. "[The character] fights back and gives as good as she gets," Knightley said. "Why would you want to be the simpering maiden in the corner when you could be hitting people in the head?"*

Pirates of the Caribbean: The Curse of the Black Pearl

Knightley's next prominent role came in the Disney blockbuster *Pirates of the Caribbean: The Curse of the Black Pearl* (2003). Knightley beat out 75 other young actresses for the part of Elizabeth Swann, who is kidnapped by a gang of pirates because of the magical medallion she possesses. Elizabeth's secret admirer, young blacksmith Will Turner (played by Orlando Bloom), enlists the assistance of pirate Captain Jack Sparrow (played by Johnny Depp) to rescue her. But instead, Elizabeth ends up rescuing Will. Knightley remarked that 20 years ago, "my character would have been a damsel in distress, . . . probably tied up a couple of times and get rescued by the boys. . . . [This character] fights back and gives as good as she gets." Indeed, that feisty spirit is why the character appealed to her. "Why would you want to be the simpering maiden in the corner when you could be hitting people in the head?"

Pirates was a big-budget Hollywood film, but expectations were modest before it debuted in July 2003. It was based on a Disney theme-park ride and was competing for moviegoers' attention against installments in several successful film franchises, including *Charlie's Angels, Legally Blonde, The Matrix, The Terminator,* and *X-Men*. In addition, pirate movies had been box-office disappointments for the past 20 years. Even the actors were uncertain about how it would do in theaters. "We all thought it was going to . . . tank," Knightley said about the wildly successful film. "I remember sitting at a screening with Orlando, going, 'Just smile through it. United front. It's gonna be all right.'"

Pirates of the Caribbean: Curse of the Black Pearl surprised critics and audiences, however, with its inventive action, sense of fun, and appealing lead actors, especially the antics of Johnny Depp as Captain Jack Sparrow. It earned over $300 million in the U.S. and $653 million worldwide, making it one of the top three films of the year, and one of the top 30 films of all time. It also made Knightley into an international star.

"What I love about acting is moving on quite quickly. It's ships passing in the night, this profession, which is kind of romantic. I became an actress to change as much as possible, that's what makes it fun."

The actress finished off 2003 with a part in the successful British ensemble romantic comedy *Love Actually.* The film starred many of Britain's most famous actors—including Knightley's childhood idol, Oscar-winner Emma Thompson—and followed several romances between loosely connected characters. Knightley played a young bride who discovers her husband's best friend is unfriendly not because he dislikes her, but because he is in love with her. The R-rated film earned $62.5 million in Britain alone, and $245 million worldwide. At the end of this breakout year, Knightley was only 18 years old, yet her films had taken in almost $1 billion worldwide.

Although Knightley was now an undeniable star, many critics still reserved judgment on whether she was more than just a pretty face. The young actress responded by taking on a wide variety of roles to show her acting skills. In *King Arthur* (2004), she was cast as the title character's love interest, Guinevere. In more familiar versions of this legend, Guinevere is merely one side of a love triangle between King Arthur and his best friend Lancelot. In this film, however, Guinevere is a warrior princess who battles to save her British homeland against Saxon invasion in the fifth century. Knightley trained in boxing, fighting, horseback riding, and archery four days a week for three months before filming started. She worked so hard she didn't need a stunt double. As a result, "Knightley has little trouble per-

Knightley as Guinevere in King Arthur.

suading one to accept the spirited future queen as an action heroine," according to *Variety* reviewer Todd McCarthy. He added that she "rivets the attention whenever she's onscreen, showing every sign of a real star in the making."

Knightley had a smaller role in her next film, the psychological thriller *The Jacket* (2005). She co-starred with Oscar-winner Adrian Brody, who played a Gulf War veteran who seems to travel through time. Knightley played a struggling waitress whom Brody's character first encounters as a little girl. Although the director was hesitant to cast her, she won him over with a believable American accent—and her desperation to play a part in something other than a costume drama. "I'm not good when people go, 'You're amazing, you're perfect for this role.' I think you've really got to fight for stuff." Although the film was only a modest success at the box office and earned middling reviews, several critics praised Knightley's performance as a believable stretch from her old roles.

Pride and Prejudice

Knightley next appeared in another costume drama—*Pride and Prejudice* (2005), based on the beloved 19th-century novel of the same name by Jane Austen. Knightley had loved the book since she was seven years old;

Knightley as Elizabeth in Pride and Prejudice.

she even bought a dollhouse of the hero's mansion with one of her first acting paychecks. In this story of the five Bennet sisters, Knightley played Elizabeth. The story follows the lively, quick-witted Elizabeth's growing relationship with the rich but proud Mr. Darcy, even as misunderstandings seem to destroy their chance for happiness together. "The beauty of Elizabeth is that every woman who ever reads the book seems to recognize herself, with all her faults and imperfections," Knightley said. With that kind of part, "if you give an actress who is even remotely good the chance to play a fantastic character like that, they are going to revel in it."

Knightley still wasn't sure if she was that kind of "remotely good" actress in *Pride and Prejudice.* Seeing herself play Elizabeth on screen, "I can pick it apart completely. The way I speak, the way I look, the way I move, anything." Most critics, however, warmly praised her performance. *Entertainment Weekly* reviewer Owen Gleiberman called it a "witty, vibrant, altogether superb performance," explaining that Knightley makes Elizabeth's relationship with Darcy believable by playing her "not [as] a feminist but [as] a confused, ardent girl charting her destiny without a map." Knightley earned a Golden Globe nomination for Best Actress in a comedy or musical and an Academy Award (Oscar) nomination for best actress for her work *in Pride and Prejudice.* At age 20, she was the third youngest actress ever nominated for the best actress Oscar. While she didn't win either award (Reese Witherspoon's performance in *Walk the Line* earned both trophies), the nominations were reward enough. For all the critics who thought she was just a pretty face, she said, "at least [the nominations] shut them up for a while."

After finishing *Pride and Prejudice,* Knightley had only four days' rest before she began filming her next movie, *Domino* (2005). In this fictionalized biography she played the title character, a female bounty hunter named Domino Harvey. She is the daughter of a British film star and a fashion model who has turned her back on the Hollywood lifestyle to involve herself in the criminal underbelly of Los Angeles. To prepare for the role, Knightley trained for an hour a day during *Pride and Prejudice,* focusing on martial arts. Using guns was a different issue, however. "I thought I liked them, because I enjoyed doing things with swords and knives on *Arthur* and *Pirates.* . . . The reality of guns, and knowing how easy it was to pick one up and shoot somebody dead, really freaked me out." While director Tony Scott cast Knightley for her combination of beauty and toughness, critics were not entirely convinced by her performance, and the film performed poorly at the box office.

"The beauty of Elizabeth is that every woman who ever reads the book seems to recognize herself, with all her faults and imperfections," Knightley said about Pride and Prejudice. *"[If] you give an actress who is even remotely good the chance to play a fantastic character like that, they are going to revel in it."*

Returning to *Pirates of the Caribbean*

Her next film put Knightley back in the Hollywood spotlight. After the first *Pirates* film proved box office gold, she had agreed to reprise her role as Elizabeth Swann in two sequels. In the second installment, the 2006 blockbuster *Pirates of the Caribbean: Dead Man's Chest,* Elizabeth is about to marry sweetheart Will Turner when they are arrested and imprisoned for treason, for aiding the escape of the swaggering Captain Jack Sparrow. They face execution unless they locate Sparrow and his magical compass, which leads to a buried treasure chest. This task is made more difficult by the sinister and ghostly Davy Jones, a monstrous blend of man and squid, and his ghoulish followers.

When writing about the new movie, many critics faulted its two-and-a-half-hour running time as too long, its plot as overly convoluted, its special effects as excessive, its gags as repetitive, and Depp's performance as over the top. But audiences couldn't get enough. *Dead Man's Chest* earned $135.6 million in its first weekend alone — a record in the U.S. — on its way to taking in over $420 million total from American audiences. Worldwide, the film earned just over $1 billion, making it the third highest-grossing film of all time (behind *Titanic* and *Lord of the Rings: Return of the King*).

Fans around the world eagerly await the third installment of the series, *Pirates of the Caribbean: At World's End,* which is scheduled to be released in May 2007. According to director Gore Verbinski, the final film will bring the unfolding romantic drama between Will and Elizabeth to a climax. "They realize love is something that hurts," Verbinski said, "and there are things they have to overcome if the relationship is to last."

"

According to director Gore Verbinski, the final Pirates *film will bring the unfolding romantic drama between Will and Elizabeth to a climax. "They realize love is something that hurts," Verbinski said, "and there are things they have to overcome if the relationship is to last."*

"

Filming the two *Pirates* sequels took up much of Knightley's time in 2005 and 2006. Still, the actress found time to complete two other movies for release in 2007. One is the historical drama *Silk,* based on the bestseller by Italian novelist Alessandro Baricco. The film focuses on a 19th-century silk merchant who travels from France to Japan and embarks on a forbidden affair. Knightley plays the merchant's wife, who gradually becomes aware of her husband's romantic obsession. She is also scheduled to appear in *Atonement,* based on Ian McEwan's novel set in Britain during the 1930s and 1940s. Knightley plays Celia, a girl whose relationship with a young servant leads to tragedy when her younger sister misinterprets it. The actress also has plans to star in *The Best Time of Our Lives,* a script written by her mother, Sharman Macdonald. The story is set in the mid-20th-century and deals with the complex relationship between Welsh poet Dylan Thomas and his childhood friend, Vera Phillips, the role Knightley is slated to play. Knightley has said that acting in one of her mother's works will fulfill a longtime dream.

Knightley has been in the acting business for more than a decade and shows no signs of slowing down. Part of that is due to her parents. "I'm

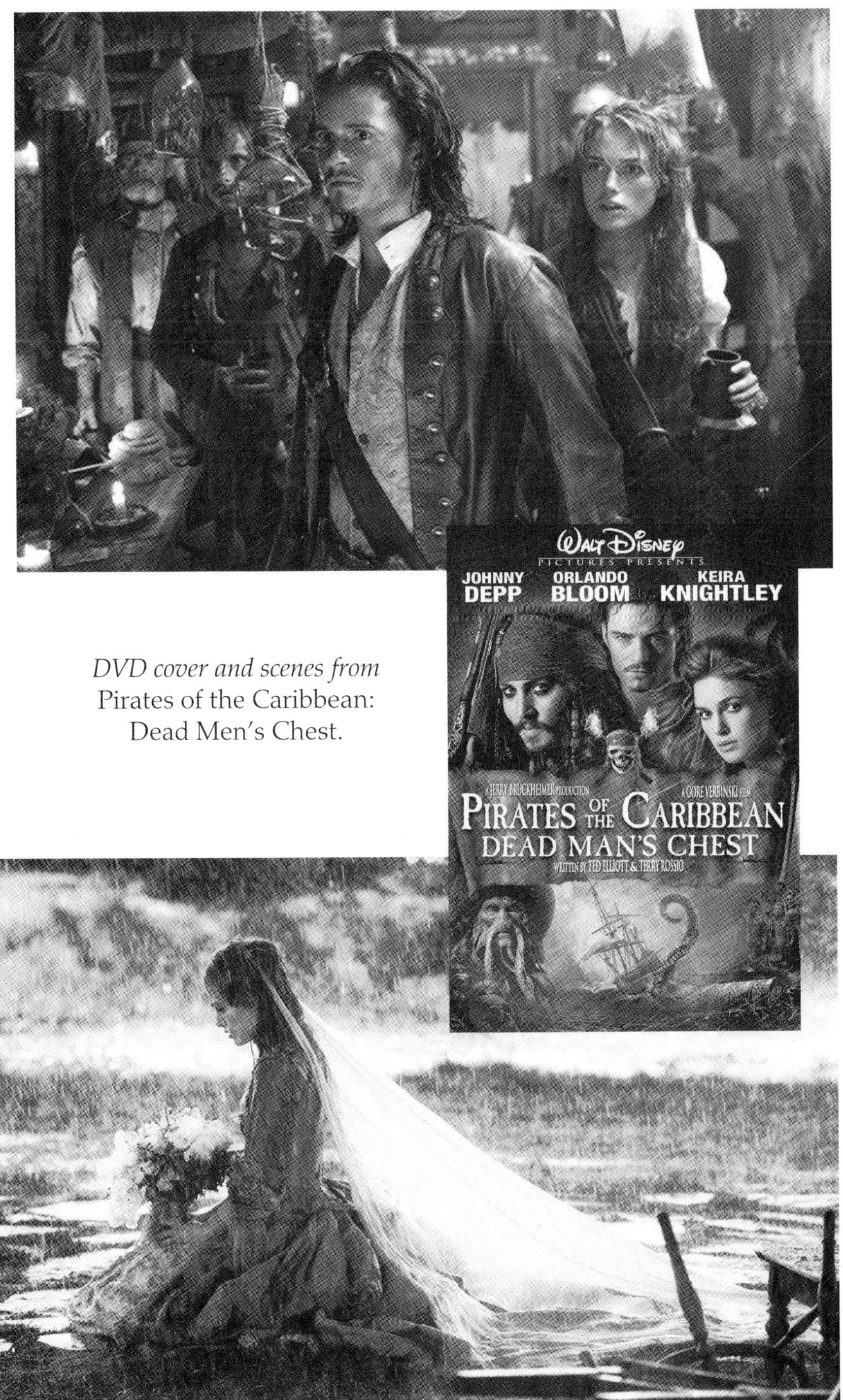

DVD cover and scenes from Pirates of the Caribbean: Dead Men's Chest.

the daughter of a theater actor and a playwright and I know this is a job that blows down even quicker than it blows up. All you can do is ride the wave while it's there and enjoy it." She expects that some day "the work is going to dry up, and people will get bored of me. That's not bitterness, just the truth." Nevertheless, she hopes to keep working as an actress. "What I love about acting is moving on quite quickly. It's ships passing in the night, this profession, which is kind of romantic. I became an actress to change as much as possible, that's what makes it fun." If she can make films that move people, that would be the best reward. When she was growing up, "there was a sense that my parents' work was important and that it could change the world in a way. That's an amazing thing to be around. It's inspiring. It makes you want to be great."

——— " ———

"You can't make yourself anything you're not. If you're going to be thin, that's fine. But if you're not, that's fine. Celebrate whatever shape you are."

HOBBIES AND OTHER INTERESTS

Knightley's busy filming schedule leaves her little spare time, but when she is home she enjoys cooking. She roots for West Ham United, a soccer team in the English Premier League. When she goes out, she enjoys art galleries and shopping, with shoes being her favorite indulgence. She also likes experimenting with creative arts such as drawing, painting, and photography.

Knightley's striking good looks and acting success have brought her endorsement deals with British luxury jeweler Asprey and Chanel's Coco Mademoiselle fragrance. But she also uses her image to benefit charities. In 2005, she posed for publicity photos on behalf of WaterAid, a charity dedicated to providing safe drinking water and sanitation in Africa and Asia. She also lent her image to the American Library Association's "Read" campaign, appearing in a poster connected to *Pride and Prejudice.*

Knightley's physical appearance has certainly won her many admirers, but it has also made her the focus of some controversy. As she has become more popular, she has become a regular feature in fan magazines, where photographs show that she has gotten noticeably slimmer. The actress has admitted that her grandmother and great-grandmother struggled with anorexia, but she has denied rumors that she has an eating disorder. She attributes her slender figure to genetics and a healthy diet and tries not to obsess over it. "You can't make yourself anything you're not. If you're going to be thin, that's fine. But if you're not, that's fine. Celebrate whatever shape you are." Still, after photographs were widely published in which she appeared to be dangerously thin, many have become concerned about her weight and her health.

HOME AND FAMILY

Knightley owns an apartment in London, which she sometimes shares with friends and her brother Caleb. Despite her success, she doesn't have a personal manager or assistant. As a young adult, she explains, "you're meant to be growing up and handling things on your own." The actress gets advice from her family instead: "They're fantastically supportive but also highly critical. I prefer that to somebody completely [sucking up to] me." When she films far away from home, her mother sometimes joins her on location.

Knightley, who is single, has said that that her busy work schedule leaves her little time for relationships. The actress refuses to comment on her personal life, except to say that she does not get involved in on-set romances with co-stars. Occasionally some of her on-set friendships have developed into romances after shooting ended, and she has been linked with young actors from England and Ireland.

SELECTED ROLES

Television Films

Royal Celebration, 1993
Treasure Seekers, 1996
Coming Home, 1998
Oliver Twist, 1998 (miniseries)
Princess of Thieves, 2001
Doctor Zhivago, 2002 (miniseries)

Movies

A Village Affair, 1994
Innocent Lies, 1995
Star Wars: Episode I—The Phantom Menace, 1999
The Hole, 2001
Bend It Like Beckham, 2002
Pure, 2002
Pirates of the Caribbean: The Curse of the Black Pearl, 2003

Love Actually, 2003
King Arthur, 2004
The Jacket, 2005
Pride and Prejudice, 2005
Domino, 2005
Pirates of the Caribbean: Dead Man's Chest, 2006

HONORS AND AWARDS

Best Newcomer Award (London Critics Circle): 2003, for *Bend It Like Beckham*
Best International Actress Award (Irish Film and Television Festival): 2004
Breakthrough Award (Hollywood Film Festival): 2004
Variety UK Personality of the Year (British Independent Film Awards): 2005

FURTHER READING

Books

Contemporary Theatre, Film, and Television, Vol. 38, 2002
Hurst, Brandon. *Keira Knightley,* 2006

Periodicals

Biography Magazine, Dec. 2003
Boston Globe, Nov. 6, 2005, p.N13
Elle, Aug. 2006
Entertainment Weekly, Nov. 18, 2005, p.102
CosmoGirl, Aug. 2006, p.128
Cosmopolitan, Aug. 2004, p.44
Current Biography International Yearbook, 2005
Los Angeles Times, July 6, 2003, part 5, p.12; Mar. 5, 2006, p.E7
Sunday Times (London), Oct. 2, 2005, Features p.4
Time, July 5, 2004, p.84
Times (London), Sept. 10, 2005, p.22
USA Today, July 4, 2003, p.D2
Vanity Fair, April, 2004, p.314
Variety, July 6, 2004, p.4; Nov. 21, 2005, p.C2
Vogue, Dec. 2005, p.318; May 2006, p.222

Online Articles

http://www.elle.com/coverstory/9029/keiraknightley.html
(Elle Magazine, "Shining Knightley," July 18, 2006)
http://www.wateraid.org/international/about_us/newsroom/3060.asp
(WaterAid, "Keira Knightley Takes the Plunge for WaterAid," Jan. 15, 2005)

Online Databases

Biography Resource Center Online, 2007, article from *Contemporary Theatre, Film, and Television,* 2002

ADDRESS

Keira Knightley
Endeavor Agency
9601 Wilshire Boulevard
Beverly Hills, CA 90201

WORLD WIDE WEB SITES

http://www.foxsearchlight.com/benditlikebeckham
http://disney.go.com/disneyvideos/liveaction/pirates/main_site/main.html
http://www.prideandprejudicemovie.net/splash.html
http://disney.go.com/disneypictures/pirates

Sofia Mulanovich 1983-

Peruvian Surfer
2004 World Champion Female Surfer

BIRTH

Sofia Mulanovich was born on June 24, 1983, in Lima, Peru. Her father, Herbert Mulanovich Barreda, is a seafood exporter. Her mother, Ines Aljavin de Mulanovich, is a restaurant owner. Sofia is the second of three siblings. Her brother Herbert, Jr., is four years older than Sofia and is a national surfing champion. Matias is three years younger than Sofia and is also pursuing a career in competitive surfing.

YOUTH

Mulanovich grew up in the small coastal village of Punta Hermosa, located about 30 miles outside Lima, the nation's capital. She describes Peru as "a beautiful country in South America. We have the mountains where it rains a lot and it is super cold. But it is full of really amazing things to see, such as Machu Picchu which is an old temple built by the ancient

Incas. There is another region of Peru which is all jungle and extremely hot all year long and full of native people and mysteries."

Mulanovich is also proud of Peru's rich cultural heritage, including its status as the possible birthplace of the sport of surfing. Pottery that was made in the region more than 1,500 years ago depicts surfers. Some historians believe that this evidence suggests that the sport may have originated in Peru rather than Hawaii, the area that is usually most identified with surfing. Scholars also note that in the mid-20th century, a wealthy Peruvian named Carlos Dogny played an important role in popularizing surfing beyond the Hawaiian Islands. Dogny founded the elite Waikiki Surf Club in Lima in 1942, and another surf club in Biarritz, France, a short time later. Dogny's clubs not only helped make the sport a worldwide one, but also influenced generations of the Mulanovich family. Sofia Mulanovich's grandfather and her father were both members of the prestigious Waikiki Club.

"I just loved it," Mulanovich said of her early years of surfing. "It was easy for me. [The surf] was right there in front of the house. I open one eye and I see the waves."

Living on the coast and growing up in a family that was so enthusiastic about surfing, Mulanovich learned how to handle herself in the water at a very early age. She began swimming when she was just three years old. By the age of five she was using a bodyboard—a small foam board that can be ridden on waves while kneeling, lying down, or standing up. By the age of nine, she had graduated to a small surfboard known as a shortboard. The size of these boards makes it hard to catch big waves, but they are considered easier to maneuver than a standard board, so they are ideal for beginners.

When Mulanovich first started surfing, she was informally coached by Roberto Meza, one of Peru's top surfers. Meza took her to a beach called Cerro Azul to get her started. "She tried to stand up but fell the first few times," Meza recalled. "But before the day was over, she stood up and went for a long ride. Not many can do that on their first day."

"I just loved it," Mulanovich said of her early years of surfing. "It was easy for me. [The surf] was right there in front of the house. I open one eye and I see the waves." At the time, Mulanovich was one of few females hitting the waves, but she did not mind that. She routinely tagged along with her older brother and other boys who surfed, building her own skills by watching them and informally competing against them. When she was not out in the ocean riding waves, she spent much of her free time studying surf videos for inspiration and technical insight.

Ocean Provides Refuge from Violence

Mulanovich's parents encouraged her interest in surfing. They knew their daughter was safer riding the waves with her brothers and her friends than she would have been nearly anywhere else. Peru was a dangerous place in the early 1990s, boiling with political problems and related violence. Kidnappings, bombings, and murders happened nearly every day in Lima and other large cities. "We were really frightened to go anywhere, to the bank, to the malls, the movies and restaurants," remembered Sofia's mother, Ines Mulanovich. "People were killed every day."

Fortunately, Mulanovich's parents had the financial resources to protect their family in ways that poorer families could not. For example, Mulanovich and her brothers attended expensive private schools in Lima rather than the dangerous public schools, and they were transported to and from their home in bulletproof vehicles. "Sofia was very young at that time," recalled Ines Mulanovich, "and fortunately it was not very shocking for her as it was for us adults."

Insulated from the violence swirling around her, Mulanovich was able to focus on her dream of a career in professional surfing. "When I first stood on a surfboard I knew I wanted to be a pro surfer," she remembered. Roberto Meza continued to be one of her mentors, and as her skills developed, she was coached by another Peruvian surfing great, Magoo de la Rosa. Their guidance helped her make a big splash in amateur surfing competitions, which had no separate categories for girls and women. "I actually loved surfing against the boys," she remembered. "They were funny when I beat them."

Even though there were many fine surfers in Peru, however, there was no surf industry to support and sponsor them. "Peru is a really poor country and there is not much support or organization in any sport besides soccer," Mulanovich explained. "We try to improve it, but it is really hard to make things happen when the country's economy is so bad." This knowledge convinced her parents to allow her to go to Guadalupe, Mexico, at age 12 to attend a major Pan American surfing competition. She was there merely to observe and get the feel of high-level competition, but Mulanovich also impressed onlookers with her aggressive, fluid, powerful moves in the water.

EDUCATION

During her youth in Lima, Mulanovich attended a British-run, private school for girls called the San Silvestre School. "Peru is a poor country, but it is divided into sectors. The lower sector kids go to public schools which have terrible education because they don't have money enough to pay good teachers. The other sector has private schools which are really expensive but they give you an insane education," she explained. Of the San Silvestre School, Mulanovich said that "the worst part was that it was only for girls! It was a nightmare sometimes, but now I am thankful because I had great teachers and I can say that I learned a lot of things."

CAREER HIGHLIGHTS

Mulanovich's surfing career began in earnest in 1996, when the 13-year-old sensation was recommended for a place on the Peruvian surfing team by Roberto Meza and Magoo de la Rosa. Later that year, she made her debut at the top level of surfing competition at the U.S. Open at Huntington Beach, California. She even faced the reigning women's world champion, Layne Beachley, in one of her first heats. Mulanovich made it all the way to the quarterfinals before being eliminated. (For more information on Beachley, see *Biography Today Sports,* Vol. 9.)

> *"I actually loved surfing against the boys," Mulanovich remembered. "They were funny when I beat them."*

One year later, Mulanovich represented her country at the Pan American competition, held in the Caribbean. Geoff Moysa, a member of the United States team at that time, remembered watching the newcomer surf and said, "We were all tripping on this tiny little girl who was just ripping—tons of speed and really aggressive. Everyone knew right away she was the real deal." After competing in the U.S. Open again that year, Mulanovich complained about having to leave the competition in order to get back to school in Lima: "I'm not looking forward to that," she said. "I want to stay and surf. It's so cool here."

Teen Surf Star

In 1998 Mulanovich won the Pan American championship in Brazil at the stunningly young age of 15. Her growing stardom received another boost after the release of a surf documentary called *Blue Crush.* The film, produced by Bill Ballard (not to be confused with the 2002 Hollywood surf movie *Blue Crush*), was a showcase for talented female surfers, including Mulanovich, Keala Kennelly, Kate Skarratt, Rochelle Ballard, and Sanoe Lake. *Blue Crush* eventually became one of the best-selling surf documentaries of all time. It was featured in five film festivals and sold in more than 45 countries. Although Mulanovich was only a teenager, her power and style were evident in the film.

Analyzing her own style, Mulanovich notes that she is what surfers call a "regular footer," meaning she rides with her left foot forward (someone who rides with their right food forward is known as a "goofy foot"). "My body is what makes me a good surfer," she adds. "Being short . . . I have a low center of gravity, which helps me drive power through my legs and initiate turns faster. Feeling my legs and abs tightening and the board turning in response — that's the best feeling for sure, because it reminds me how strong I am. I've watched my body become more powerful as I've surfed; it's adapted to what I have to do. As an athlete, I use my body to express myself. Without surfing, I wouldn't be me!"

"My body is what makes me a good surfer," said Mulanovich. "I've watched my body become more powerful as I've surfed; it's adapted to what I have to do. As an athlete, I use my body to express myself. Without surfing, I wouldn't be me!"

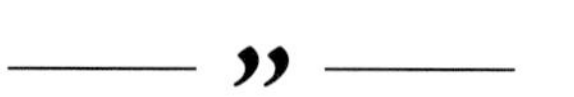

Mulanovich acknowledges, though, that despite her fast and powerful surfing style, the greater body strength of men naturally allows them to achieve more in surfing than most women can hope to do. "I love watching the boys surf but we will never be as good as them. . . . Men are men and women are women and the boys are always going to surf better and that's a fact."

Surfing on the World Championship Tour

Mulanovich ranked as Peru's female national surfing champion from 1999 to 2002. During this time, she was increasingly treated as a national hero, someone that Peruvians could feel good about after so many years of trouble and violence in their country. Her success also brought her a wave of new endorsement deals. In 2001, for example, she reached a deal with Roxy, the womenswear division of sportswear manufacturer Quiksilver.

Mulanovich at the World Championship Tour Roxy Pro competition in Hawaii, 2001.

This endorsement deal gave her the funding she needed to enter the World Qualifying Series (WQS) for the first time.

The WQS is the doorway to the World Championship Tour (WCT), the highest level of surfing competition, sanctioned by the Association of Surfing Professionals (ASP). In the WCT, the 18 top surfers travel around the world for 10 months of the year, living and surfing together and competing against one another for the world championship. In her first year in the WQS competition, Mulanovich finished second overall and missed qualifying for the WCT by only one position.

In 2002 Mulanovich remained with the WQS but took advantage of several opportunities to compete in wildcard slots in WCT events. The first was the World Championship Tour Roxy Pro competition on Australia's Gold Coast. She had won the chance to surf there by defeating 15 rivals at a trial competition. According to one writer for the *Gold Coast Bulletin,* Mulanovich performed at the trials "with a style and savagery rarely seen in women's surfing." Mulanovich also won two other wildcard spots in WCT events that year. She then closed out the 2002 season with a third-place finish at the WQS Turtle Bay Resort Women's Pro event in Hawaii. This performance, combined with her record for the rest of the season, qualified her to surf as a regular with the WCT in 2003.

Mulanovich at the World Championship Tour Roxy Pro competition in Australia, 2002.

Hungry and Humble

By 2003 Mulanovich was well-known to even the top competitors of the world surfing community. Surfing legend Layne Beachley, for example, commented that she was "typical of the young guns around the tour now. Most of them have the power to pull off men's moves. They also have nothing to lose and are unpredictable, which can make them more daunting to surf against than the seasoned competitors."

Other members of the tour described Mulanovich as a humble, kind person as well as an incredibly talented athlete. "Sofia is always looking for ways not to stand out," said Megan Abubo of Hawaii. "If she wins a contest, she just wants to be part of the gang and hang with her friends. She is so cool. She never makes you feel bad if she wins and you lose, and she never says anything bad about anyone." Mulanovich became particularly close friends with Chelsea Georgeson, a surfer from Australia's Gold Coast who is the same age.

Mulanovich surfed well in 2003, her rookie season on the WCT tour. She turned in her best performance at the November Roxy Pro in Hawaii, the first of three contests in the so-called women's triple crown of surfing. She was the first Peruvian ever to win this prestigious event. On her first wave she scored a 7.0 out of a possible 10, turning five times on a left-handed wave. Next, she earned a score of 8.0 for performing three top-to-bottom carves on a four-foot wave. "She was killing it," said competitor Melanie Bartels, who placed second that day. "I would watch her when I was sitting out there and she was throwing big chunks [of water]. Real impressive."

The 2003 season was a dream come true for Mulanovich. "Traveling with friends, surfing contests, and surfing good waves is great. I'm having the time of my life right now," she said. "Traveling has its ups and downs but everything is like that, so I have to always keep positive and never lose focus. I have felt lonely many times because in a way I am different from everybody else on tour; different language, culture, and sometimes beliefs. Yet in many ways, we are all the same; we love surfing and we have the same dreams and ambitions. It is hard to be far from away from family and my country but I love what I am doing and I am conquering new experiences and feel good about life."

> *"Traveling with friends, surfing contests, and surfing good waves is great. I'm having the times of my life right now," Mulanovich said. "Traveling has its ups and downs but everything is like that, so I have to always keep positive and never lose focus."*

World Champion

In 2004, at the age of 21, Mulanovich realized her lifelong dream. She took the gold at the 2004 World Surfing Games in Salinas, Ecuador, won the Fiji Roxy Pro in April, and racked up more wins at events in Tahiti, France, and the United States. By the end of the tour, she had triumphed over Layne Beachley, who had held the world champion title for six consecutive years. Mulanovich was crowned the 2004 World Champion female surfer, the first ever to come from Latin America.

Not surprisingly, Mulanovich's victory boosted her celebrity status in her native Peru to even greater heights. Billboards around the country displayed pictures of the star surfer, huge crowds greeted her when she made public appearances, and a monument was erected in front of the National Stadium to honor her. Yet despite the adoration from her fellow Peruvians, Mulanovich remained as humble and unpretentious as ever. "Sofia's popularity is due not only to her success as a world champion,

Mulanovich at the World Championship Tour Roxy Pro competition in Hawaii, 2006.

but to her simplicity, naturalness and modesty that she always carries with her," declared her press agent, Hans Firbas. "She is one of us, and the people admire her for it."

In 2005 Mulanovich faced a new challenge—defending her world championship. Her keenest competition came from her best friend, Chelsea Georgeson. The rivalry between the two was intense throughout the 2005 season, with each winning key victories. In the end, Georgeson triumphed over Mulanovich by a narrow margin, taking the world championship from her friend. Mulanovich was unable to reclaim the championship crown in 2006, but she did win the U.S. Open at Huntington Beach for the first time in her career.

Mulanovich remains one of the world's top surfers, and she is confident that she can reclaim her former spot at the top of her sport. Mulanovich stated that her future plans are to "keep surfing, try to improve myself as a surfer and a human and just enjoy the ride." She reflected that achieving those goals also requires a commitment to taking good care of herself: "I never forget that I have a goal in life and whatever I do I have to make sure it is not ruining my mind nor my body because I will need both in order to follow my path."

In 2006 Mulanovich's career became the subject of an award-winning documentary film titled *Sofia: A Documentary.* It explores the background of terrorism and political violence in Peru, chronicles her rise to surf star, and looks at her influence on the surfing industry and on Peru in general. Mulanovich has also been featured in the surf documentaries *Peel: The Peru Project, Shimmer, Modus Mix,* and *MUVI 2,* which was made by Mulanovich herself.

HOME AND FAMILY LIFE

Mulanovich is single and travels with the WCT for 10 months of the year, but has her own condominium at Punta Hermosa in Peru, a short distance from her family's home. She remains close to her parents and her brothers.

HOBBIES AND OTHER INTERESTS

Mulanovich is a big music fan who counts Bob Marley, UB40, The Doors, and Carlos Vives as particular favorites. She also enjoys surf videos and documentaries so much that she has begun exploring filmmaking herself. Other interests include backgammon, jogging, dancing, and playing tennis. "It is really good to keep your mind and body active all the time," she explained. "I also watch what I eat because I want to be loose on my board and super fast. I like salads and fish and I hate junk food."

> *"Sofia is always looking for ways not to stand out," said fellow surfer Megan Abubo. "If she wins a contest, she just wants to be part of the gang and hang with her friends. She is so cool. She never makes you feel bad if she wins and you lose, and she never says anything bad about anyone."*

SELECTED HONORS AND AWARDS

ASP Rookie of the Year (Association of Surfing Professionals): 2003
Surfer Magazine Video Award for Best Wipeout: 2003
WCT Champion Female Surfer (World Championship Tour): 2004
ESPY Award for Best Female Action Sports Athlete (ESPN): 2005

FURTHER READING

Books

Current Biography International Yearbook, 2004

Periodicals

Los Angeles Times, Aug. 5, 1997, p.C8; Feb. 28, 2005, p. D1; Oct.7, 2005, p. D11
Miami Herald, Nov. 1, 2004, p.A13
Teen People, Mar. 1, 2006, p.110

Online Articles

http://www.surflifeforwomen.com/
(*Surf Life,* "Pro-File, Sofia Mulanovich," 2003)
http://www.transworldsurf.com/surf/
(*SURF Magazine,* "Girls Gone Wild: Sofia Mulanovich," Sep. 23, 2004)

ADDRESS

Sofia Mulanovich
Mosaic Sports Management
2033 San Elijo Avenue #102
Cardiff-by-the-Sea, CA 92007

WORLD WIDE WEB SITES

http://sofiamulonovich.com
http://www.aspworldtour.com

Jamie Oliver 1975-

British Chef and Cookbook Author
Star of TV Cooking Shows and School Nutrition Activist

BIRTH

Jamie Trevor Oliver was born on May 27, 1975, in Clavering, a small village in Essex, England. His parents, Sally and Trevor Oliver, own a pub-restaurant in Clavering called The Cricketers. Sally manages the business end of their establishment, while Trevor runs the kitchen. Oliver has one younger sister, Anna-Marie.

YOUTH

Throughout his early life, Oliver was surrounded by cooking and restaurants. He grew up above the family pub, and his first job there was cleaning up and taking out the garbage. He began peeling potatoes and shelling peas when he was about seven or eight. His mother remembered his enthusiasm for cooking at an early age: "We used to stand him on a chair so that he could reach the work surface and obviously he used to get into a real mess—he still uses his hands for everything when he's cooking!" Oliver's father had a strong work ethic, and he taught his son the value of getting up early. If Oliver slept late on the weekend, his father would "squirt me [with a garden hose] through the window to wake me up and tell me that people die in bed."

"I remember being fascinated by what went on in the kitchen," Oliver said. "It just seemed such a cool place, everyone working together to make this lovely stuff and having a laugh doing it. . . . A lot of the boys at school thought that cooking was a girlie thing I didn't really care."

For Oliver, one incentive for working for his parents was the pocket change he earned. He knew that some people—his friends included—thought cooking was women's work, but he considered himself one of the boys in the kitchen, working with the male chefs his parents employed. "I remember being fascinated by what went on in the kitchen. It just seemed such a cool place, everyone working together to make this lovely stuff and having a laugh doing it. . . . A lot of the boys at school thought that cooking was a girlie thing. I didn't really care, especially as I could buy the coolest trainers [tennis shoes] with what I'd earned from working at the weekend."

Oliver experienced a lot of early success in the kitchen, which inspired him to keep cooking. At age 13, he was sent by his father to work part time at Starr, a finer restaurant than The Cricketers. Oliver hadn't had any formal training in cooking yet. Within a few weeks, he replaced a 26-year-old chef who couldn't prepare the appetizers as well as he could. According to Oliver, hearing his dad tell him he was proud of him left him feeling "all tingly and funny."

Another episode in Oliver's early life inspired him to keep cooking. He and his friends would take sandwiches with them on escapades into the countryside on summer days. Oliver prepared smoked salmon sandwiches one day, and a friend who only ate jam on bread reluctantly took a bite of the fancier fare. "He really didn't want to eat it, and then, when he did, he wouldn't eat anything else all summer. That's when I understood how powerful food can be," Oliver said.

EDUCATION

Oliver was popular in school, but he struggled academically. He has dyslexia, a learning disability that is an inherited neurological condition. People with dyslexia have trouble recognizing and decoding words, which can make reading, writing, and spelling difficult. People with dyslexia often have trouble with reading comprehension.

At the age of 16, Oliver was accepted at Westminster Catering College in London. Having done poorly in local schools until then, going to cooking school brought him long-awaited academic success. "The course was a perfect mix of practical and theory, which suited the type of person I am. I can pretty much take anything in as long as I can see it. We didn't just sit there reading out of a book, which is basically why I failed at school. Even when it was pretty hardcore science, like growing bacteria and learning how it affects kitchens, it was fine because it related straight to cooking."

FIRST JOBS

After finishing his studies at Westminster Catering College, Oliver spent several years trying different experiences and jobs to learn all about cooking. First he went to France to soak up more cooking knowledge. Then he returned to London to work as the head pastry chef at The Neal Street Restaurant, a renowned establishment where he became fascinated with Italian food. After reading a cookbook by Rose Gray and Ruth Rogers, Oliver sought out a job at their London restaurant, the critically acclaimed River Café. He spent over three years there, learning more about Italian food from the proprietors. "Those two ladies taught me all about the time and effort that goes into creating the freshest, most honest, totally delicious food."

CAREER HIGHLIGHTS

"The Naked Chef"

One night while Oliver was working at the River Café, a crew from the TV network the British Broadcasting Corporation (BBC) showed up at the restaurant to film a documentary. Without even trying, Oliver stole the

Oliver in a shot from his TV show "The Naked Chef," squeezing lemon on his food.

show. "I didn't even know they were filming me in particular. We were all working, and I was just doing my thing. Because it was so busy . . . there wasn't even any room to be polite to them, much less perform for the camera," he recalled. Still, his "performance" impressed many in the television industry, and five different production companies called him when the documentary aired. All wanted to develop a cooking show for him. Oliver was surprised: "I couldn't believe it and thought it was my mates winding me up!"

It took some convincing before Oliver agreed to do a cooking show. "Being a restaurant chef, my industry feeling was TV chefs are idiots and cheesy geezer cop-outs and my dream is to open my own restaurant," he recalled. Being an active participant in the development of his own show, which had a rock 'n' roll soundtrack, made the decision easier. The show was called "The Naked Chef," although Oliver didn't like the title. "I was worried about what my nanny (grandma) would think—like I was a bloody porn star or something!" The title of the show actually referred to his philosophy of cooking good food with high quality ingredients and basic techniques. "The idea behind 'The Naked Chef' was to strip food down to its bare essentials—to prove that you didn't need to dress up ingredients or buy a load of fancy gadgets to make something really tasty."

"The idea behind 'The Naked Chef' was to strip food down to its bare essentials—to prove that you didn't need to dress up ingredients or buy a load of fancy gadgets to make something really tasty."

Oliver's enthusiasm and skill made for popular television when "The Naked Chef" first aired in 1999. As a critic for the *Observer* noted, "Jamie Oliver was a breath of fresh air. Within months he was one of the most popular personalities in the country." The show had Oliver riding his scooter around London, searching for ingredients and sharing his passion for food with shop owners and fishmongers. He could hardly contain his excitement as he cooked, jumping about the kitchen and sliding down a banister to let in his friends for his on-air dinner parties.

The success of "The Naked Chef" as a TV show prompted Oliver to write a cookbook of the same name. "I always wanted to write a book, though I doubt my old English teacher would believe it!" His success inspired two more series and accompanying cookbooks. The TV shows "Return of the Naked Chef" and "Happy Days with the Naked Chef," along with the

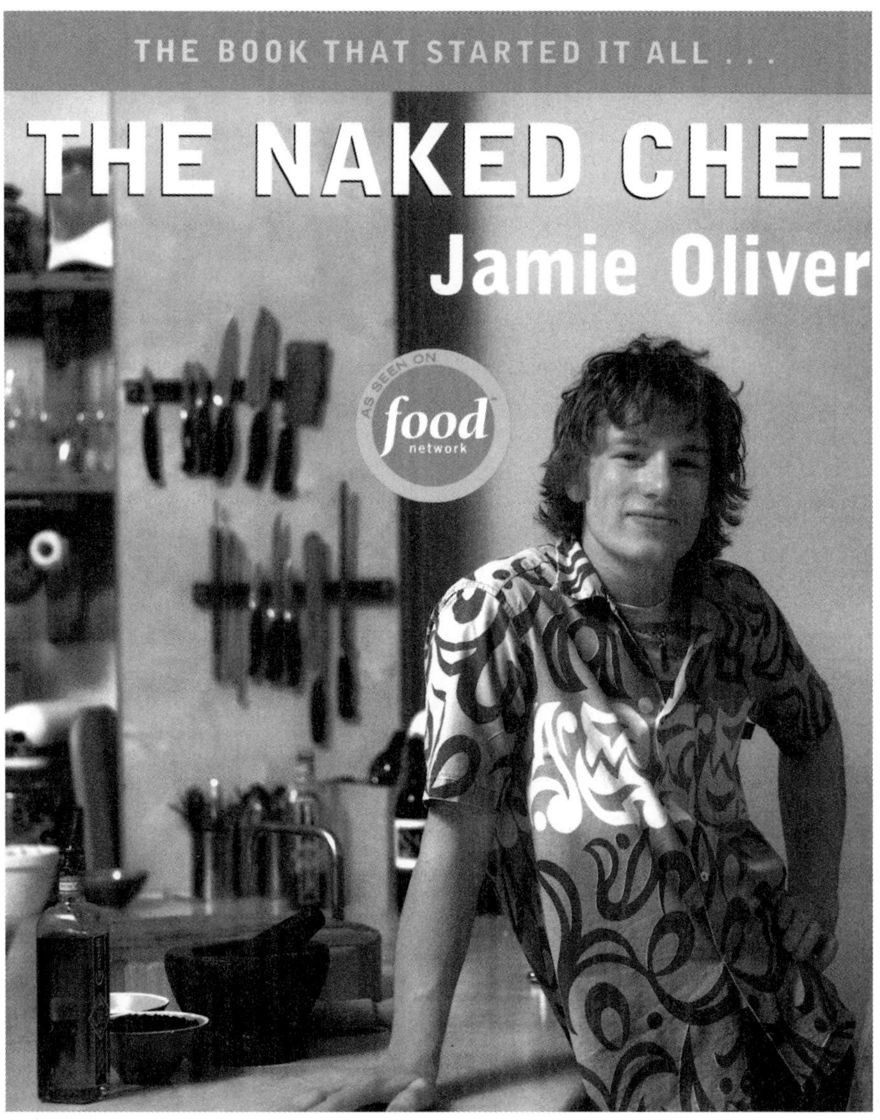

cookbooks of the same names, made Oliver a rich and busy chef. Since then, he's gone on to do a number of other cookbooks based on his experiences in the kitchen.

Fifteen Underprivileged Youngsters

In 2002, Oliver started a new project: he came up with a plan to train 15 troubled teens how to cook. Using his own money, he developed a course for these kids and, along with many of his friends and colleagues, set about teaching them everything about the cooking and catering business. Once they completed the class, the 15 graduates were responsible for running Oliver's new restaurant, aptly named Fifteen. Most of his students had no chef's training, and some had never eaten in a restaurant. Oliver explained, "Essentially, the trainees are unemployed but most of them are also coming from the same classes I did at school—not academic. The course is about second chances. Half the kids who had attitude problems didn't have steady families and have experienced drug or alcohol abuse. How do you expect these kids to get a break if no one offers them one?"

Oliver felt that the 15 teens he chose for his program needed something positive to focus on, and what better than food? His own passion for cooking was something he wanted to share. "For me, cooking is like breathing," he said. "I look forward to breakfast when I go to bed, I look forward to lunch, I look forward to dinner, I look forward to a dinner party in two weeks' time. I honestly, truly, truly think cooking is an integral part of life, of having fun. I don't eat to live, I live to eat."

“

"For me, cooking is like breathing," Oliver said. "I look forward to breakfast when I go to bed, I look forward to lunch, I look forward to dinner, I look forward to a dinner party in two weeks' time. I honestly, truly, truly think cooking is an integral part of life, of having fun. I don't eat to live, I live to eat."

"Jamie's Kitchen," a TV miniseries about the London group's experience, revealed both successes and failures when it aired in 2002. Several students lost interest, while a few others were asked to leave the program due to disciplinary or attendance problems. Many support programs were available to the students, including mentoring, counseling, and a ten-year plan with provisional backing for a business once they'd gotten that far. But some could not step up to the challenge of long hours and demanding instructors.

Despite the failure of some of the kids, Oliver recruited a second group to train. "Early on," he admitted, "I think I was a bit too careful not to offend anyone and I had this optimistic belief that the kids would all be all right in the end. I probably needed to be harder on them. I am harder on them now!" During the second course, he learned more about being a mentor and relished the difference he was making in his trainees' lives. "I'm perfectly happy. I get my pleasure out of the students. That's becoming a stronger part of why I do it. 'Fifteen' is not some airy-fairy TV show. It's for life," he said.

The London restaurant Fifteen is still in operation. It is owned by the Fifteen Foundation, a not-for-profit group for which Oliver is a trustee. The foundation has established Fifteen restaurants in Amsterdam, Cornwall, and Melbourne. Profits from the restaurants go back to the foundation to fund development.

"Everyone now is looking round schools talking about the food in the kitchen, and that alone keeps schools on their toes," Oliver said. "But I'm worried that sufficient money hasn't filtered through to our glorious dinner ladies, who are the grass roots of the whole thing. Deep down, I don't know how much better off they are a year later."

Improving School Food

Oliver's charitable attention turned next toward British schoolchildren and what they were eating at school. He was concerned about the low nutritional value of school lunches and thought that kids would change their eating habits if they learned more about good food and fresh ingredients. He knew that dietary changes would help children lead healthier lives, especially important given that obesity rates had drastically increased over recent years. "Basically, I wanted to get rid of the junk," Oliver said.

The "Feed Me Better" campaign began in one school district in Greenwich, England. The district fed 15,000 children every day at dinner (lunch in the U.S.). Oliver gathered the head dinner ladies and taught them the basics of fresh food preparation. Previously the dinner ladies had been simply heating up prepared foods that arrived at the schools in bags, cartons, and cans.

The kids did not react well at first. The healthier fare tasted strange and they longed for the comfort of their familiar crisps (potato chips) and fizzy drinks (soda). The *New York Times* reported on student reactions: "'It looks disgusting and it smells disgusting,' said one student, confronted by Mr. Oliver's chicken tagine (stew). Another little boy, tasting what he said was his first-ever vegetable, threw up on the table." But the program was ulti-

Oliver's efforts to improve the eating habits of British schoolchildren were captured in a 2005 film documentary.

mately a winner: most children eventually grew to like the new cuisine, teachers reported a rise in academic performance and concentration, and parents commented on their children's improved behavior. To help some of the younger kids along, Oliver donned a corn-on-the-cob costume, sang a tune about vegetables, and handed out stickers.

Oliver filmed a TV documentary called "Jamie's School Dinners" showing the trials of the dinner ladies and the reactions of the schoolchildren in Greenwich. Once the documentary aired in 2005, an impressive number of people signed his petition to the government for better nutrition in British schools. Oliver argued for several important changes in his "Feed Me Better Campaign": guaranteeing that children receive nutritionally balanced meals; introducing nutritional standards and banning junk food from schools; supporting dinner ladies by giving them better kitchens, more work time, and more training; teaching kids about food and nutrition; and committing long-term funding to improve school food. Oliver's campaign was a great success. Prime Minister Tony Blair set up a School Food Trust and pledged over $500 million to improve school meals. New standards were put in place for school food, and school junk food sales were banned. Oliver called it "20 years too late. . . . [The government should be] bloody embarrassed that London has some of the most unhealthy children in Europe."

Oliver putting the finishing touch on a dessert.

A 2006 follow-up documentary, "Jamie's Return to School Dinners," showed Oliver in various parts of the country, checking up on schools and the changes that had been made. While many schools had made drastic improvements, others continued to struggle with outdated kitchen facilities and limited funds for cafeteria operations. "The subliminal ripples, especially through the middle class, have been fantastic," Oliver reported. "Everyone now is looking round schools talking about the food in the kitchen, and that alone keeps schools on their toes. But I'm worried that sufficient money hasn't filtered through to our glorious dinner ladies, who are the grass roots of the whole thing. Deep down, I don't know how much better off they are a year later."

Recent Projects

Oliver has continued to tackle a wide range of projects related to food and cooking. In summer 2005 he had the opportunity to explore one of his long-time passions. He has been enamored of Italian food for most of his career, so he set off across Italy to uncover the secrets of authentic Italian cooks. He drove an old Volkswagen bus, which broke down repeatedly, and had a camera crew follow him on his adventure. "Jamie's Great Italian Escape" was a six-part miniseries that showcased Oliver's passion for food, its preparation, and the people who appreciate it. He recalled the journey on his website: "I had a great time exploring the delights of the busy night markets in Palermo, entering pasta making competitions with the mammas in the small mountain community in Le Marche and injecting some enthusiasm into cooking for the Benedictine community north of Rome." Oliver's tribute to Italy was his cookbook *Jamie's Italy*, published after his experience.

Oliver returned to the original group of 15 student chefs from "Jamie's Kitchen" in "Jamie's Chef," a TV miniseries that aired in 2007. After the original experience, he had hoped that one of his students would open their own restaurant. Oliver decided to give them that chance. He invited the group to a competition, where each presented their best dishes to a panel of judges from the foundation. The judges picked four chefs, who had to prove themselves in the kitchens of some of London's best restaurants. It was a grueling experience, but one lucky and talented winner will get the opportunity to open his or her own restaurant.

> *"People who press olive oil, grow tomatoes, dive for scallops, pig farmers who breed rare pigs and feed them on chestnuts and herbs and produce the most amazing pork . . . these people are all fantastically brilliant," Oliver raved. "I accredit all of my success to these people for giving me the inspiration for what I do."*

MARRIAGE AND FAMILY

Oliver married Jools (Juliette) Norton, his childhood sweetheart, in 2000. They have two daughters, Poppy Honey and Daisy Boo. As Oliver's family has grown, so has press fascination with his private life. When their first daughter was born and they were getting ready to leave the hospital, Oliver and Jools realized they could either embrace the waiting horde of photographers or flee, and they chose to face the press. "The hospital offered to smuggle us out the back, but we knew that as well as all the mob out front, there were already five paparazzi outside our house with long lenses that could see in through the windows. . . . So we said, OK, we'll be out around 3:30 tomorrow. And when we came out, they were the politest I'd ever seen them—they kept saying, 'Congratulations!'"

MAJOR INFLUENCES

Oliver is appreciative of and inspired by the people who provide the food he cooks. "People who press olive oil, grow tomatoes, dive for scallops, pig farmers who breed rare pigs and feed them on chestnuts and herbs and produce the most amazing pork. . . . These people are all fantastically brilliant and, whether you like it or not, it's infectious," he said. "I accredit all of my success to these people for giving me the inspiration for what I do."

SELECTED CREDITS

Television

"The Naked Chef," 1999 (series)
"Return of the Naked Chef," 2000 (series)
"Happy Days with the Naked Chef," 2001 (series)
"Jamie's Kitchen," 2002 (miniseries)
"Oliver's Twist," 2002-2003 (series)
"Jamie's School Dinners," 2005 (documentary)
"Jamie's Great Italian Escape," 2005 (miniseries)
"Jamie's Return to School Dinners," 2006 (documentary)
"Jamie's Chef," 2007 (miniseries)

Writings

The Naked Chef, 1999
The Return of the Naked Chef, 2000
Happy Days with the Naked Chef, 2001
Jamie's Kitchen, 2002
Jamie's Dinners, 2004
Jamie's Italy, 2005
Cook with Jamie, 2006

Videos

"The Naked Chef," 2000
"Pukka Tukka," 2000
"The Naked Chef—Volume Two," 2001
"Happy Days Tour Live!," 2002
"Oliver's Twist," 2003
"Jamie's Kitchen," 2004
"Oliver's Twist—Volume Two," 2005

"Jamie's School Dinners," 2005
"Jamie's Christmas," 2005
"The Naked Chef, Series 1-3," 2006 (boxed set)

HONORS AND AWARDS

Man of the Year (*GQ*): 2000
Best Chef of the Year (*GQ*): 2000
BAFTA (British Academy of Film and Television Arts): 2001, for "The Naked Chef"
Member of the British Empire (MBE): 2003
National Television Awards: 2005 (two awards), Most Popular Factual Programme for "Jamie's School Dinners" and Special Recognition Award

FURTHER READING

Books

Current Biography International Yearbook, 2005

Periodicals

Caterer & Hotelkeeper, Nov. 27, 2003, p.22
Daily Telegraph (London), May 13, 2006, p.1 (Weekend section)
Guardian (London), Sep. 24, 2005, p.18
New York Times, Apr. 23, 2005, p.A4
Observer (London), Apr. 14, 2002; Mar. 26, 2006, p.22; Aug. 22, 2006, p.1 (Features section)
People, Nov. 13, 2000, p.107
USA Today, Apr. 2, 2001, p.D1
Vogue, May 2006, p.260

Online Articles

http://www.bbc.co.uk/food/food_matters/schoolmeals.shtml (British Broadcasting Corporation, "School Dinners," Sep. 2006)

Online Databases

Biography Resource Center Online, 2007

ADDRESS

Jamie Oliver
Enquiries
PO Box 51372
London N1 7WX
England

WORLD WIDE WEB SITES

http://www.jamieoliver.com
http://www.fifteenrestaurant.com
http://www.foodnetwork.com/food/jamie_oliver

Michael Sessions 1987-

American Politician
Elected Mayor of Hillsdale, Michigan, at the Age of 18

BIRTH

Michael Sessions was born on September 22, 1987, in Goshen, Indiana. He lived the first six years of his life in Nappanee, Indiana, before moving to Hillsdale, Michigan, with his family. His father, Scott Sessions, is a medical technician, and his mother, Lorri Sessions, is a housekeeper for a sorority house at Hillsdale College. He has a younger sister, Sarah.

YOUTH AND EDUCATION

Sessions attended Gier Elementary School and Davis Middle School in Hillsdale. He was an inquisitive and active youngster. "I think I was really hyper as a kid," he said. "I was always occupied with something."

While Sessions was growing up, current events and politics were frequent topics of conversation around the dinner table. "Dad always had an opinion and he always voiced it," he recalled. His early interest in politics was further sparked in the fourth grade, when his class took a field trip to the state capitol in Lansing. He was fascinated by the hustle and bustle of the lawmakers as they debated various measures and voted on important state business. By the end of the day, he decided that he wanted to learn more about how elected officials dealt with the problems and challenges of running a government.

Over the next several years, Sessions read about politics and even attended political rallies, including a local rally for then-presidential candidate George W. Bush in 2000. He also decided to study the local political scene in his hometown of Hillsdale, a community of 8,200 people located about 100 miles southwest of Detroit. "He would watch the town City Council meeting on TV every week," his mother said. "He'd try to get us to join him. He found the whole process fascinating."

Sessions attended Hillsdale High School, where he played football, ran cross country, and was a member of the track team. "I was an above average student," Sessions said, "in the A's and B's range." His favorite subject was history. In the afternoons, he often worked as a volunteer tutor at the middle school. Meanwhile, his interest in politics continued to grow. During his senior year, he ran for vice president of the student council and lost. Undaunted, Sessions turned his attention to a much bigger office—the mayorship of Hillsdale.

CAREER HIGHLIGHTS

Sessions's keen interest in local politics was driven in large part by his belief that the city's elected officials had not done enough to attract and keep manufacturing businesses in the area. In 2003, for example, a local automobile manufacturing plant had closed and moved its operations to Mexico. Sessions's father, who had been a plant supervisor, was one of the local residents who found himself out of work as a result of the plant closure. Scott Sessions was unemployed for two years before he completed his retraining as a medical technician. The period of his father's joblessness was "horrible," Michael Sessions recalled. "It just hits the family hard—the lack of money. The lack of being able to do stuff like before. Coming home and figuring out, well what are we going to put on the table?"

In spring 2005 Sessions learned that the city's incumbent 51-year-old mayor, Douglas Ingles, was running unopposed in the upcoming November election for another four-year term. "I thought, 'you can't generate many new ideas for the city of Hillsdale without the whole campaign process,'" Sessions recalled. "So I decided to throw my name into the race.'"

Throwing His Hat into the Ring

When Sessions called the city clerk and asked about filing papers for his candidacy, he was told that at 17, he was too young to be a legal candidate. In September 2005, though, Sessions registered to vote on his 18th birthday. By that time, the deadline had passed for him to get his name on the ballot. Rather than give up, however, Sessions filed papers with the city clerk to become a write-in candidate for mayor. The position of mayor in Hillsdale is nonpartisan, which means the candidates do not run as a member of a political party. The position is a part-time one that comes with a $3,600 salary but no office or staff. The mayor's responsibilities include presiding over two City Council meetings a month, where policy and budget decisions are made. Day-to-day administration of the city's affairs is carried out by the city manager.

"[Sessions] would watch the town City Council meeting on TV every week," his mother said. "He'd try to get us to join him. He found the whole process fascinating."

Sessions made the decision to run for mayor without talking to his family. When he told his parents of his candidacy, they were very surprised. "'You're crazy! You're crazy, Michael,'" he recalled them saying. "They weren't angry. They were skeptical as to what I was doing. [I told them] 'I really want to do this and I'm going to do it, Mom and Dad.'"

Once they saw how serious Sessions was about his candidacy, his parents firmly supported him. But it was up to Sessions to organize and finance his campaign himself. He used the $700 he had earned from a summer job working for a concessions company to purchase business cards, as well as window and lawn signs. Admitting that he was "not very good

Sessions being sworn in as mayor of Hillsdale, Michigan.

with slogans," he ordered simple signs that said: "Write in Michael Sessions for Mayor." He put the signs up all over the city and began knocking on doors to introduce himself. "Each day after school, he would pick an area and go door to door, telling people who he was and that he was running for mayor," recalled Lauren Beck, a friend who helped him with his campaign. "He'd talk about why he should be mayor, and had a sample of the ballot so he could show people where they had to write in his name."

Residents who found Sessions at their doorstep often asked how old he was. Most of them were startled to learn that the candidate was an 18-year-old high school senior. At first, many people thought that his candidacy was a hoax or a scheme to bolster his college application. But as Sessions persisted, many people expressed admiration for his spirit and sense of civic duty. Those who showed a willingness to hear what he had to say often came away impressed by his grasp of current events and his deep affection for Hillsdale. His teachers, meanwhile, expressed pride in his campaign. According to Peter Beck, the assistant principal of Hillsdale High School, "He's not our smartest kid. He's not our best athlete. He's just an ordinary kid with some big goals. He's a closer. He gets the job done."

Sessions organized town hall-style meetings at the Kiwanis Club, a record and coffee shop, and the local firehouse so residents could ask him questions. At each of these events he laid out his plan for the city, which included attracting more jobs, turning an old factory into a bio-diesel plant, and forming a stronger partnership with nearby Hillsdale College. His pledge of support for increasing the Hillsdale fire department from three to four full-time members earned him his first high-profile endorsement, from the Hillsdale City Fire Association.

In the weeks leading up to Election Day, Sessions kept up a demanding schedule of campaigning and school. But the pressure of being a full-time student and a candidate finally wore him down. Five days before the election, he came down with a severe case of bronchitis. His mother blamed his illness on long hours of campaigning outside in the cold. "I tried to tell him to wear a coat," she said, "but he wouldn't."

"Each day after school, he would pick an area and go door to door, telling people who he was and that he was running for mayor," recalled Lauren Beck, a friend who helped Sessions with his campaign. "He'd talk about why he should be mayor, and had a sample of the ballot so he could show people where they had to write in his name."

Celebrity Mayor

The Hillsdale mayoral election took place on November 8, 2005. When the final votes were counted, Sessions was declared the winner, by a two-vote margin of 670 to 668. "It's amazing," he said after his victory had been officially recognized. "I'm so excited, I think I'm going to be ill."

The victory made Sessions one of the youngest mayors in the United States and sparked a flood of media interest in the young man and his community. Dozens of reporters flocked to Hillsdale to ask the mayor-elect about his triumph. He also made appearances on several television shows, including "The Today Show," "Countdown with Keith Olbermann," and "Late Night With David Letterman." Sessions flew to New York City with his parents to appear on Letterman's show, where he participated in the show's famous "Top Ten" segment by reading a list prepared by the show's comedy writers called "The Top Ten Reasons to Be An 18-Year-Old Mayor." Two of Sessions's favorite jokes on the list were: "Every night, a different member of the town council does my homework," and "Parents try to tell me what to do, I raise their taxes."

Sessions's unlikely rise to mayor even attracted interest from foreign media outlets. More than 20 camera crews from as far away as Japan and Russia traveled to Hillsdale to record his swearing-in ceremony. Astounded by the coverage, Sessions asked a Japanese reporter why he was interested in him. The reporter answered that "age equals wisdom." Recalling that conversation in a speech to a youth group, Sessions remarked, "That's the thing about America. We don't necessarily believe that age equals wisdom. We think youth can make a difference."

Once the media interest in his victory subsided, Sessions was able to refocus on his high school studies and begin his mayoral duties. For the remainder of his senior year, his typical weekday began with high-school classes from 7:40 in the morning to 2:30 in the afternoon, followed by a meeting with Hillsdale's city manager to discuss various municipal business. He also made a point to get out in the community and meet with constituents and business owners. "I never want to call a business and find out they're leaving because the city wasn't listening," he explained. To make time for his new schedule, however, Sessions had to make some sacrifices. He reluctantly quit all after-school activities. "I am quite good with time management and managing my time, which you have to be in this situation," he said. "I really lay out what my priorities are and go and attack them."

"In government, everything starts locally," Sessions remarked. "Folks, there are a ton of things that can be done in your community. Whether it is washing windows in downtown or volunteering at the senior center. We as young people have the power to change the world and ourselves."

Sessions earned his high school diploma in spring 2006, as scheduled. He then enrolled at Hillsdale College, where he is studying politics and economics. Even as he shoulders a college workload, though, he is continuing with all his mayoral duties. Sessions reserves most evenings for city-related business, including the bimonthly City Council meetings. Afterwards, he heads home to do his college work. He tries to get to bed before midnight, but Hillsdale city manager Tim Vagle notes that the mayor is not always successful. "I get emails from him at 1 in the morning," Vagle told the *Christian Science Monitor*. "I mean, when does he sleep?"

Sessions has adopted a wait-and-see attitude regarding a future career in politics. "I'm taking it one step at a time," he said. But his experiences

Sessions leading a city council meeting.

have deepened his conviction that every person has a civic obligation to try to improve his or her community. He believes that this obligation extends to young people, even if they have not yet reached voting age. "In government, everything starts locally," he remarked. "I love to take the quote from John F. Kennedy and change it to fit what I think. I always tell young people to, 'Not ask what their community can do for them, but what they can do for their community.' Folks, there are a ton of things that can be done in your community. Whether it is washing windows in downtown or volunteering at the senior center. We as young people have the power to change the world and ourselves."

HOME AND FAMILY

Sessions still lives at home with his parents and sister, with just a short drive to Hillsdale College. He uses his bedroom as both an office and a study area. Sessions may be in charge of city council meetings, but he notes that "my parents still have the final say in the house."

FURTHER READING

Periodicals

Christian Science Monitor, Apr. 3, 2006, p.20
Detroit News, May 8, 2006, p.A1

Junior Scholastic, Feb. 20, 2006, p6
People, Junior Edition, Feb. 20, 2006, p.107
Los Angeles Times, Nov. 11, 2005, p.A1
New York Times, Dec. 15, 2005, p.F1
Toledo (OH) Blade, Nov. 22, 2005, p.A1

Online Articles

http://abcnews.go.com/GMA/story?id=1296769
(ABC News, "High School Senior Elected Mayor of Mich. Town," Nov. 9, 2005)
http://www.crfforum.org/topics/?topicid=42&catid=8
(CRF Forum, "Governance: An Interview with Michael Sessions," June 7, 2006)
http://hillsdale.net/stories/112205/news_sessions001.shtml
(The Hillsdale Daily news online, "Sessions Takes City's Reins," Nov.22, 2005)
http://hillsdale.net/stories/060706/news_20060607015.shtml
(The Hillsdale Daily news online, "For Teen Mayor, It's on to College," June 7, 2006)
http://www.msnbc.msn.com/id/10004343/
(MSNBC, "18-year-old Mayor Taking His New Job Seriously," Nov. 9, 2005)
http://www.statenews.com/article.phtml?pk=36875
(The State News, "Meet 18-year-old Michael Sessions . . .the Mayor of Hillsdale," July 14, 2006)

ADDRESS

Michael Sessions, Mayor
Hillsdale City Hall
97 North Broad Street
Hillsdale, MI 49242

WORLD WIDE WEB SITE

http://www.ci.hillsdale.mi.us/sessions.htm

Kate Spade 1962-

American Fashion Designer
Creator of Distinctive Purses and Other Accessories

BIRTH

Kate Spade was born Katherine Noel Brosnahan in 1962 in Kansas City, Missouri. She was the fifth of six children in a close-knit Irish Catholic family. Her father worked for a family-owned construction business that built many of the roads and bridges around Kansas City. Her mother was a full-time homemaker to Kate, her two sisters, and three brothers.

YOUTH

Kate Brosnahan was raised in Kansas City, where her parents gave her a practical Midwestern upbringing. Although part of a large family, she still enjoyed one-on-one time with her mother. She treasured mother-daughter visits to a local chocolate shop, where she indulged in Napoleon-style pastries. "It was kind of our time together, and it seemed so special," she recalled.

Kate recalls that she was interested in fashion when she was young, but she wasn't obsessed with it. "When I was a kid, I didn't even know Chanel," the famous French fashion company (pronounced "shuh-NELL"). "I would have called it 'Channel.'" Wanting to distinguish herself from her two sisters, young Kate learned to develop her own style. As a teenager she hunted through local thrift shops for vintage clothes. She learned to appreciate classic styles from the 1950s and 1960s, as embodied by two of her style icons, actresses Audrey Hepburn and Grace Kelly. "My mother thought it was great because a lot of what I was buying were like things she used to wear." Kate also discovered she loved bright colors, such as kelly green and raspberry pink.

"

"I was not obsessed with [fashion]," Kate recalls. "When I was a kid, I didn't even know Chanel [pronounced shuh-NELL]. I would have called it 'Channel.'"

"

EDUCATION

After graduating from high school in Kansas City, Kate Brosnahan entered the University of Kansas. She later transferred to Arizona State University, where she studied journalism and broadcasting. She graduated with a bachelor's degree in 1985.

MARRIAGE AND FAMILY

Kate Brosnahan met fellow student Andrew Spade while at Arizona State University, when the two of them worked in the same men's clothing store. Kate moved to New York City shortly after finishing college, and Andy joined her there in 1988, taking a job at an advertising company. They became business partners in 1993, and got married the following year. In February 2005 they had a daughter, Frances Beatrix. The couple splits their time between New York City and their cozy 1870 cottage in Southampton, New York.

Kate and Andy Spade in the front row of a fashion show in New York City.

CAREER HIGHLIGHTS

From Style Reporter to Style Maker

After graduating from college and taking a tour of Europe, Spade moved to New York City. She shared a two-bedroom apartment with three other girls and managed to get an internship at *Mademoiselle* magazine in 1986. Her first duties included fetching coffee at photo shoots, but she soon worked her way onto the magazine's editorial staff. By 1991 she was a senior editor in charge of accessories, which meant she investigated and wrote about the latest trends in jewelry, purses, and shoes.

Despite her expertise, though, Kate found that she had trouble finding a handbag that appealed to her own personal sense of style. Almost all the purses she saw were made of black or brown leather, while she liked bright colors and different textured fabrics. "I wanted a functional bag that was sophisticated and had some style," she explained. When she thought she might like to leave journalism and work for herself, Andy encouraged her to try creating her own handbags. By then they were sharing a small apartment in SoHo, a trendy neighborhood in Manhattan in New York City; he agreed to support them both for a year while Kate tried her hand at design.

With no background in manufacturing, Kate had a lot to learn before constructing her first handbags. She started with some simple sketches and paper patterns, then checked with producers around New York City to see how much they would cost to make. She cashed out her retirement savings account to fund production, and in 1993 she left her job to focus on her business—but only after asking her boss if they would take her back if she failed. She remembered that "even my mother said I'd gotten cocky—and what the heck was I doing giving up a job with insurance?" Those she encountered in the fashion business weren't very encouraging, either. She remembered that one fabric supplier told her, "Honey, you look like a nice girl. You don't want to get into the business. Settle down." With Andy's support, Kate persisted in the face of discouragement: "Not knowing much about the fashion industry kept me from being nervous," she said. "It kept me from being intimidated."

Kate found it reassuring to work with her husband. "Knowing your best interest and the company's best interest is in the forefront of every decision being made without you is really comforting," she explained.

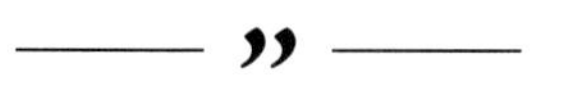

By 1993, the designer was ready to present her bags at a New York accessories show. She considered several names for the label, but finally settled on a combination of her first name and partner Andy's last name. Her first collection, which she called "kate spade," included just six styles of handbags. These boxy but stylish tote bags were made of practical fabrics like nylon, burlap, and linen. Their simple shapes and colorful patterns recalled the classic era of 1950s and 1960s fashion. At that first show she made a sale to Barney's, a local department store, but it didn't cover her expenses. "It was kind of a loss," she recalled. "I thought, 'It didn't work out and now we have to stop.'" The handbags generated such positive buzz, though, that Andy became convinced she was on the verge of success. Before their second show, Kate removed tags from the inside of the bags and sewed them to the outside. The simple black labels, which said "kate spade—new york," charmed fashion editors and led to more sales.

In late 1993, Kate and Andy brought in Pamela Bell as a partner handling production, and in 1994 Kate's old college friend Elyce Arons joined as a partner overseeing sales and public relations. In these early days the couple's small studio apartment was also their workshop; when it was shipping time, they had to find somewhere else to sleep. Cash was even more scarce than space, and Kate and Andy (who married in 1994) had to draw on their own personal savings to buy fabric and pay employees. Luckily, kate spade handbags were gaining more attention: they appeared in more stores, including Bergdorf Goodman, Saks, and Bloomingdale's, and they were featured in fashion magazines and on the arms of several Hollywood celebrities. Revenues grew from $100,000 in 1993 to $1.5 million in 1995, the same year they moved the company into a new space in New York City's flower district.

The year 1996 saw the company, named Kate Spade Inc., achieve several milestones. The company made a profit for the first time, on overall sales of $6 million. Andy made the decision to leave his advertising job and work full-time for the company, becoming creative director and chief executive officer (CEO). Kate found it reassuring to work with her husband. "Knowing your best interest and the company's best interest is in the forefront of every decision being made without you is really comforting," she explained. In 1996 the company also opened its first kate spade store, in New York City's trendy SoHo district. Besides selling merchandise in its own store, the company sold 3,000 bags each to the Saks and Neiman Marcus chains that year. Their year of success was crowned when Kate won a New Fashion Talent Award for Accessories from the prestigious Council of Fashion Designers of America (CFDA).

Growing a Successful Company

Now that the company was profitable, the Spades worked to increase their business. They moved their flagship store to a larger SoHo location in fall 1997. That year they also opened their first international store, in Japan. In 1998 they expanded further, opening a second U.S. store in Boston and introducing a line of stationery. Kate explained their philosophy in going beyond handbags: "We won't license the name or expand into a new area unless we think we can bring something new to a category that makes it fresh." She picked stationary for her new line because traditional notebooks, diaries, personal organizers, and address books were so dark and plain that she wanted to create brightly colored, stylish, and feminine products that wouldn't look out of place in a kate spade handbag. By the end of 1998 the company had earned nearly $30 million in total sales, and Kate was named Best Accessory Designer of the Year by the CFDA.

In early 1999, the Spades and their partners sold a 56% stake in the company to luxury department store chain Neiman Marcus for $33.6 million. They also expanded the scope of their business, introducing their first line of shoes and branching out into men's accessories with a JACK SPADE store in New York City. JACK SPADE gave Andy the chance to explore his

Spade shown with a few of her fashionable accessories.

own design ideas, emphasizing high quality products that combined functionality and style. Kate received another honor in 1999 when New York's Cooper-Hewitt Museum (the Smithsonian Institution's national museum of design) included some of her handbags in their first national design triennial celebrating American design excellence.

In 2000 the Spades continued building on their success by adding stores in Chicago, Illinois; San Francisco, California; Greenwich, Connecticut; and Manhasset, New York. The following year they expanded their product line into eyeglasses, both prescription and sunglasses. Then in 2002 they paired with cosmetics giant Estee Lauder to launch "kate spade beauty," a line of bath and body products that included a signature fragrance of white floral bouquet. The line won a 2003 Fragrance Foundation Recognition Award ("FiFi" Award) for Bath & Body Star of the Year. Although they were working with other companies on these new products, Kate noted that "we want to maintain creative control over everything that goes out under our name—whether we're manufacturing it or letting a partner handle production." These expansions and partnerships were a deliberate business strategy on their part, she explained: "In the short term, it's a great way to challenge ourselves creatively while raising awareness of our brand." The strategy was working; the company, now Kate Spade LLC, had approximately $70 million in sales in 2002.

Another sign that the kate spade brand was increasingly successful was in the number of counterfeit bags that began appearing on street corners—so many that by 2002 the company had hired a specialist to fight the fakes. At one point they estimated that one fake kate spade bag was being sold for each legitimate one. They worked with authorities to seize illegal shipments and let consumers know that counterfeit sales often support organized crime. A genuine kate spade bag is not cheap—prices can range from $150 to over $500—but they cost less than some trendy, high-fashion labels and are designed to become a wardrobe staple. "If you can't keep wearing the things in our line, then we feel we made a mistake," the designer noted. Besides, she added, "I really like the idea of saving for something if you want it."

Building a Brand to Last

In its second decade as a company, Kate Spade LLC continued to develop the brand. Since 2003, the company has added boutiques in many major American cities, and it began offering sales from its website in 2004. It opened an international flagship store in Aoyama, Japan, in 2004, joining three other stores in Japan, three in Hong Kong, and one each in the Philippines and Thailand. By 2006 the company had expanded to 19 stores (plus four outlet stores) in 15 states, with products available in over 400 high-end department stores and boutiques throughout the U.S. "While we've been relatively conservative" in opening stores, Kate noted in 2005, "retail is important for what you have to say as a company. But nothing is set in stone. When you run a business, you have to be nimble to be successful. I'm not opening stores [just to open them]. We are building stores where our customers are and where they might not be getting the whole [presentation]."

———— " ————

"For better or worse, we don't do a sweeping theme for each collection. I don't shop that way, so why would I design that way? It's more about different moods," Kate explained. "[If something] will be out of style tomorrow, it won't be added to the line today."

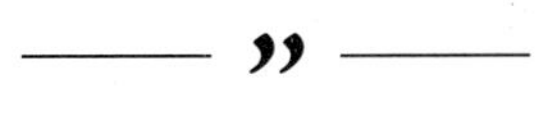

In 2004 the company branched out into items for the home, launching a collection that included bedding, bath items, china, wallpaper, fabrics, and other decorative pieces. While such practical items might seem ordinary, the designer observed that "I don't think you need to neglect the style of something that's functional." Others agreed that Spade had brought style to her new line of home products, which earned a Giants of Design Tastemaker Award from *House Beautiful* magazine, an American Food and Entertaining Award from *Bon Appetit* magazine, and an International Design Award for bedding from *Elle Decor.* For fiscal year 2004 the company generated some $125 million in sales.

The following year Kate and her husband completed a renovation of the flagship store in SoHo to display their entire line of merchandise. The store reflects her own eclectic taste: it is decorated with modern art, and in addition to kate spade products, it also offers vintage jewelry and books for sale. "I'm not afraid of experimenting with things," the designer explained. "I don't like being too tightly merchandised. Everything has a common thread. Just because I design doesn't mean I can't appreciate other people's designs. Our customers aren't going to stand still; they need some unpredictability."

For fall 2005 Kate created a new line called Collect. The line wasn't a collection of items meant to be worn together; rather, it was inspired by objects the designer herself collects. The handbags in the Collect line are made from more expensive materials, such as snake skin and beaver fur. "We were very conscious of keeping the signature collection accessibly priced," Spade noted. "But with Collect I'm allowing myself to be free and kind of unconcerned about those things. Now I'm thinking, 'Let's have fun.'" She partially attributed this new design approach to becoming a mother in 2005: "There's a bigger responsibility in place and, honestly, I'm not worrying as much. The looseness to Collect—I think it comes out of being a little more relaxed."

"I'm not afraid of experimenting with things," the designer explained. "I don't like being too tightly merchandised. Everything has a common thread. Just because I design doesn't mean I can't appreciate other people's designs. Our customers aren't going to stand still; they need some unpredictability."

Continuing Success

To date the Kate Spade company has shown no signs of slowing down. Net profits (sales minus costs) in fiscal 2005 were about $84 million, making the company an attractive purchase when Neiman Marcus, itself under new ownership, put Kate Spade LLC up for sale. In late 2006 Liz Claiborne, Inc., a clothing retailer that manages dozens of popular brands, purchased Kate Spade from Neiman Marcus for about $124 million. In announcing the purchase, the president of Liz Claiborne noted that "We are thrilled to welcome this iconic American brand into our Company. . . . Kate and Andy Spade, along with Elyce Arons and Pamela Bell, have created a terrific brand with a strong aesthetic and widespread consumer recognition. Our job now is to maintain the essence of Kate Spade while driving it to the next level."

Spade was a guest judge on the season three opening episode of "Project Runway," alongside fellow judges Nina Garcia, Michael Kors, and Heidi Klum (left to right).

When asked to analyze the reasons behind her success, Kate attributes much of it to her refusal to follow trends or worry about what's "in." When she shops for herself, "I don't fixate on what style a piece is, I buy it for no other reason than I like it." Her own wardrobe is filled with black A-line skirts, capri pants, and sweaters that she accents with color through shoes, handbags, and chunky jewelry. She often uses coats as jackets, wearing them like others might wear a cardigan. She brings the same back-to-basics approach to her designing: "For better or worse, we don't do a sweeping theme for each collection. I don't shop that way, so why would I design that way? It's more about different moods," Kate explained. "[If something] will be out of style tomorrow, it won't be added to the line today." Her designs may be nostalgic, she said, "but I don't want them to look like they came from a vintage store, because then they might as well have." While she still uses some of her original six handbag designs today, she makes them feel fresh and modern by using quirky new colors, patterns, or fabrics. It's this approach that makes kate spade products so appealing to everyday consumers, she argued: "We're not intimidating. I think some people get nervous about fashion because they find it a little scary. But fashion should be enjoyed; it shouldn't be looked at from a jaded, been-there-done-that point of view."

While Kate intends to keep designing for her company, she and her husband also have plans to branch out into other fields. They've already experimented with different media, publishing three books with her advice on *Manners, Occasions,* and *Style,* in 2004. These stylishly designed volumes combined her wit, practical sensibility, love of tradition, and classic style and taste. In 2005, the company debuted the first kate spade music CD, a collection of pop music specially commissioned from the British group Beaumont to be "a nod to '60s cocktail music with a jolt of modern glamour." Since 2001, the JACK SPADE division has produced three short films, as well as several books. Kate Spade herself has appeared on television: in 2002 she guest-starred on the sitcom *Just Shoot Me,* which was set at a fictional fashion magazine and starred her brother-in-law, comedian David Spade (Andy's younger brother). In 2006 she was a guest judge on the season three premiere of "Project Runway," a popular TV reality show and competition for designers.

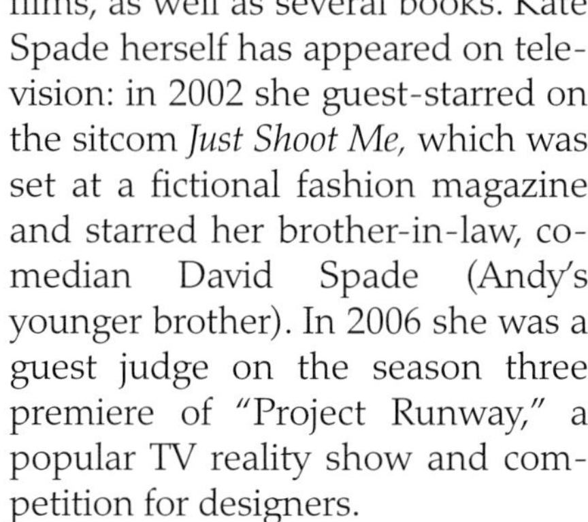

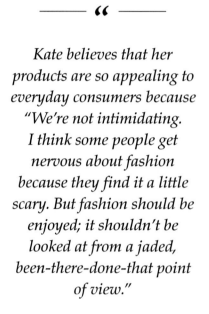

"Kate believes that her products are so appealing to everyday consumers because "We're not intimidating. I think some people get nervous about fashion because they find it a little scary. But fashion should be enjoyed; it shouldn't be looked at from a jaded, been-there-done-that point of view."

One thing that Kate doubts she ever will do, however, is move full-scale into clothing design. She has experimented with the format; in 2004 her company designed uniforms for the short-lived budget airline Song (now part of Delta Airlines) under the kate spade and JACK SPADE labels. In 2005 she collaborated with the international fashion collective As Four on a limited collection of clothing that included shrugs and trenchcoats. But when asked if she would ever create a kate spade clothing collection, the designer said: "I never say never, but I really can't imagine doing it. People are realizing accessories are important now. If I'm in the mood to shop, how fun is a great bag?"

HOBBIES AND OTHER INTERESTS

Kate enjoys relaxing at her home with her family and their Maltese terrier named Henry. She is also known for entertaining, whether planning a grand party for her husband's fortieth birthday or just a weekend with friends. When she gets away from her business on weekends, she enjoys simple pleasures of reading, walking, or biking into town to browse local shops and antique stores. She often browses flea markets to add to her collection of plates of all kinds.

Kate and her husband also use their company to support charitable causes such as Publicolor, an organization dedicated to sprucing up inner-city schools and community centers with painting projects. The Spades have created a special "publicolor" tote bag and donated 25 percent of its sales to the Publicolor project.

WRITINGS

Manners, 2004
Occasions, 2004
Style, 2004

HONORS AND AWARDS

New Fashion Talent Award (Council of Fashion Designers of America): 1996, for Accessories
Best Accessory Designer of the Year (Council of Fashion Designers of America): 1998
FiFi Award (Fragrance Foundation): 2003, Bath & Body Star of the Year, for Kate Spade Beauty

FURTHER READING

Periodicals

Fast Company, Mar. 2005, p.44
Forbes, Dec. 28, 1998, p.86
Fortune, Feb. 7, 2000, p.55
InStyle, Aug. 2002, p.272
Kansas City Star, Nov. 25, 2006, p.E1
New York Times, Mar. 12, 1999, p.B2
People, June 3, 1996, p.90
Time, Feb.16, 2004, p.36
Vogue, Aug. 2004, p.200
W, Sep. 2005, p.348
WWD, July 25, 2005, p.1

Online Articles

http://money.cnn.com/magazines/fsb/fsb_archive/2003/09/01/350794/index.htm
(CNN Money.com, "Kate & Andy Spade, Kate Spade," Sep. 1, 2003)
http://www.lizclaiborneinc.com/index2.html
(Liz Claiborne Inc. Press Release, "Liz Claiborne Inc. Agrees to Acquire Kate Spade LLC," Dec. 2006)

Online Databases

Biography Resource Center Online, 2007

ADDRESS

Kate Spade
Kate Spade LLC
48 West 25th Street
New York, NY 10010

WORLD WIDE WEB SITES

http://www.katespade.com

Carrie Underwood 1983-

American Singer
Winner of the 2005 TV Competition "American Idol"

BIRTH

Carrie Underwood was born on March 10, 1983, in Muskogee, a town in eastern Oklahoma. She grew up in nearby Checotah, a ranching community of about 3,500 people. Her father, Stephen Underwood, retired from a job in a paper mill to raise cattle. Her mother, Carole, is a retired elementary school teacher. Underwood's sisters Shanna and Stephanie were 10 and 13 years old, respectively, when she was born. They are both elementary school teachers.

YOUTH

Underwood enjoyed a happy childhood in a secure, close-knit family. "I was definitely a tomboy," she said. "I climbed trees, and I'd jump hay bales and play with the cows, and Dad would take me fishing." The Underwood children were also raised in a household that placed great importance on religious faith and ethical behavior. "I was most afraid of the 'I'm disappointed in you' speech," she recalled.

Underwood gave her first public singing performances at age three, singing songs like "Jesus Loves Me" at her family's church, the First Free Will Baptist Church. "I figured she'd make something of [her singing] because she's sung all her life," said her grandfather, Carl Shatswell. "She went to Kansas one time and was singing on the bus. Her grandmother and me, we tried to get her to hush up, but the rest of the folks on there, they wanted her to keep singing. She was just three at the time."

"

Underwood enjoyed a happy childhood in a close-knit family. "I was definitely a tomboy," she said. "I climbed trees, and I'd jump hay bales and play with the cows, and Dad would take me fishing."

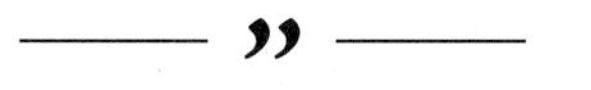

Underwood's taste in music was influenced by her parents, who loved "oldies" rock and roll songs from the 1950s and 1960s. She also picked up her sisters' taste for the so-called "hair-metal" bands that were enormously popular in the 1980s. "One of my earliest memories was singing Motley Crue's 'Smokin' in the Boys' Room' when I was five," she recalled. But she also loved the country-western music that poured out of her parents' car radio.

As Underwood grew older, she won the leads in several school musicals. She also became a regular performer at area county fairs and local Lion's Club fundraisers. She pushed her mother to take her to talent contests, though those never turned out quite as she hoped. "I competed in a lot of stuff, and I didn't win. Ever," she recalled. "That was when I was 12, 13, 14 years old. But I didn't need to win. If I got third [place] and got a little trophy or money for school, that made me happy."

When Underwood was about 14 years old, a local admirer arranged for her to go to Nashville to audition for Capitol Records. Underwood dreamed of repeating the success of LeAnn Rimes, who became a country star as a young teenager. But the audition went nowhere. "I honestly think it's a lot better that nothing came out of it now, because I wouldn't have been ready then," Underwood said. "Everything has a way of working out."

EDUCATION

Underwood was an outstanding student and Honor Society member at Checotah High School. She kept herself busy with basketball, softball, and cheerleading, in addition to her singing appearances at county fairs, school events, and church. She has described her social life during this time as wholesome and low-key. "If we were going to go out, we'd just go see a movie," she said. "We were definitely good kids. We'd all go to church together. Prom night we all went over to my friend's house and drank nonalcoholic champagne and toasted each other."

In May 2001, Underwood graduated second in her high school class, as salutatorian. "After high school, I pretty much gave up on the dream of singing," she said. "I had reached a point in my life where I had to be practical and prepare for my future in the 'real world.' " With this in mind, Underwood enrolled at Northeastern State University in Tahlequah, Oklahoma, only an hour away from home.

In college, Underwood focused on the subjects of mass communications and journalism. "I hoped to get a behind-the-scenes job in Tulsa, Oklahoma, at one of the local television news shows," she recalled. With this in mind, she gained valuable work experience by contributing to student-produced local access TV shows and the student newspaper. She also earned money for college with a variety of different summer and after-school jobs. One summer she served as a page for a state congressman in the Oklahoma House of Representatives. She also waited tables at a college pizzeria and worked for a time at a zoo and a veterinary clinic.

Underwood claims that she came out of her self-described "shy" shell during her years at Northeastern State. After joining a school sorority, She participated in various volunteer programs to collect highway litter and assist hospice patients. During the summer after her freshman year, meanwhile, she mustered up the courage to perform in the Downtown Country show, a country-western music review that included singing, dancing and comedy. This event placed Underwood on stage in front of audiences that were far larger than any she had seen during her adolescence. "It was mainly there that I learned what it was like to be in front of a crowd," she later declared.

In 2005 Underwood took a year off to make her famous run on "American Idol" and launch her musical career. But as she had promised her family, she then returned to Northeastern State University and graduated magna cum laude (with high honors) with a bachelor of arts (BA) degree in journalism in May 2006. According to Underwood, her journalism classes have been a great help to her now that she is the subject of so many interviews. "I know what the reporters are looking for [in interviews] and I also know when they're trying to make me say something bad," she said. "They'll ask me some hot-button questions, something to get myself in trouble!"

"If we were going to go out, we'd just go see a movie," Underwood said about high school. "We were definitely good kids. We'd all go to church together. Prom night we all went over to my friend's house and drank nonalcoholic champagne and toasted each other."

CAREER HIGHLIGHTS

Auditioning for "American Idol"

Underwood was a senior in college and only a few credits away from graduation when friends convinced her to audition for "American Idol," a musical talent contest that had become one of the most popular television shows in the United States since its debut in 2001. "People always told me that I should try out for the show, but I never thought I would be able to handle it," she said.

By 2005, though, Underwood realized that auditioning for the program might be a case of "now or never." "I thought, I'm about to graduate and I don't know what I'm going to do, so why not try out for 'American Idol?'" she said. "What's the worst that could happen? If I don't make it past the audition, nobody's going to know. And I'll get some experience in front of the camera." A few days later, she and her mother drove through the night for eight hours from Oklahoma to St. Louis, Missouri, where regional auditions for the show were scheduled. When Underwood arrived at 8 a.m., she joined more than 100,000 other hopefuls who were auditioning around the country. After another eight-hour wait, her turn finally came. Performing for one of the show's supervising producers, she sang a cover of Martina McBride's "Phones Are Ringing All over Town."

Underwood was sure she had blown the audition. To her amazement, though, she was invited to return the next day to sing for Nigel Lythgoe, executive producer of the program. She belted out "Independence Day," another song by McBride, one of her favorite performers. Lythgoe was

Underwood on stage with other contestants after being named the new American Idol.

sufficiently impressed to pass her on to the next stage in the competition: a performance in front of the show's infamous panel of judges, Simon Cowell, Paula Abdul, and Randy Jackson.

Standing alone in front of the panel, she delivered a spirited version of the Bonnie Raitt song "I Can't Make You Love Me." After she finished, the judges praised her sweet but powerful singing voice and her girl-next-door charm. They then gave her the news that she had been selected to compete on the 2005 version of "American Idol." A short time later, Underwood boarded an airplane for the first time in her life and was whisked off to Los Angeles.

Triumph on "American Idol"

The next several months were the most stressful of Underwood's life. "Millions of people all over the U.S. saw me do my best and my worst week to week on the show," she pointed out. In addition, her three-month adventure on the West Coast marked the first time that she had been away from home without friends or family. "[The] L.A. lifestyle was new and usually confusing to me," she said. "I learned so much on the show—about myself and about the music/television business."

When the show began, it immediately became clear that Underwood was one of the favorites. Although she was pitted against a group of 12 strong competitors, her country-music style set her apart from most of the other singers. More importantly, her talent and personality caught the attention of the judges early in the show. In one early episode, for example, acid-tongued judge Simon Cowell told her, "Carrie, you're not just the girl to beat, you're the person to beat. I will make a prediction, not only will you win this competition, but you will sell more records than any other previous Idol winner."

"

In an early episode of "American Idol," acid-tongued judge Simon Cowell told her, "Carrie, you're not just the girl to beat, you're the person to beat. I will make a prediction, not only will you win this competition, but you will sell more records than any other previous Idol winner."

"

Cowell was right. Week after week, she survived as other contestants were voted off the show. Eventually, only she and rock and roll singer Bo Bice were left. On May 25, 2005, Underwood beat Bice to become the fourth "American Idol" — and the first winner with a country music orientation. Underwood's prize package included a recording contract worth at least one million dollars and the use of a private jet for a year, as well as a Ford Mustang convertible. "Two years ago, I was at the grocery store thinking, 'I shouldn't get this cereal — the other one is a dollar less,'" Underwood marveled. "I realize how lucky I am."

A Rising Pop Star

One month after her momentous "American Idol" victory, Underwood released her first single, "Inside Your Heaven." It entered the record charts as the nation's best-selling song, establishing her as the first country-music artist ever to debut at No. 1 on the *Billboard* magazine "Hot 100" chart. The song's runaway popularity was even more remarkable because relatively few country-music radio stations aired the song.

Seizing on her red-hot popularity, Underwood secured endorsement deals for Sketchers shoes and Hershey chocolate. She also agreed to join fellow "American Idol" contestants on a 44-date concert tour that took her all around the country. Around this same time, she began laying the groundwork for her debut album, called *Some Hearts*.

Simon Fuller, creator of "American Idol" and overseer of her record contract, arranged for Underwood to take part in a weekend "writers' retreat" with some of Nashville's best song writers. During the retreat, *Some Hearts* began to take shape. It was during these sessions, for example, that "Jesus, Take the Wheel" emerged as the album's first single. "[It] was probably the first song I heard that really struck a chord with me," Underwood recalled. "The song tells such a great story."

Underwood was also struck by a song called "Don't Forget to Remember Me." "The first time I heard it, I cried because I was feeling homesick," she recalled. After her mother read the words, she called Underwood to tell her it was "our song." "In that moment, I knew that no matter how hard it would be to get through, I had to record it," she said.

Underwood helped to pick the album's material and co-wrote one of the compositions. "Writing songs is always something that I have been interested in," she said. "But I really didn't feel like my writing chops were good enough yet to write songs for my first album. I did, however, try my best to help. I wanted to help write a song that was strictly for my friends and family in my hometown of Checotah. Obviously, the name of that one ended up being 'I Ain't in Checotah Anymore.' It's basically an account of the things that have been happening to me over the past few months." Of course, the song also conveys Underwood's deep affection for her Oklahoma roots. One of her favorite lines in the song states that "I'd rather be tipping cows in Tulsa than hailing cabs here in New York."

"Two years ago, I was at the grocery store thinking, 'I shouldn't get this cereal— the other one is a dollar less,'" Underwood marveled. "I realize how lucky I am."

”

Success with *Some Hearts*

Some Hearts was released in November 2005 and went straight to the top of the charts, ranking No. 1 in country music and No. 2 in pop music. It sold 300,000 copies in the first week after its release, making it the top-selling debut record ever released by a country recording artist. Industry analysts credited the record's stunning popularity to Underwood's massive exposure on "American Idol" and its selection of songs, which appealed to country- and pop-music fans alike. Underwood acknowledged that she worked hard to please her broad fan base. "Because of the mass audience I was able to reach with 'Idol,' I wanted to make something

everyone could appreciate, not just listeners of country," she said of *Some Hearts.*

By early April 2006 *Some Hearts* had gone triple platinum, which means sales of three million copies. Underwood thus became the first female artist ever to reach the triple-platinum milestone so quickly. Meanwhile, the album's first single, "Jesus, Take the Wheel" topped *Billboard*'s Hot Country Songs chart for six consecutive weeks. Other hit singles from the album include "Don't Forget to Remember Me," "Before He Cheats," and "Inside Your Heaven."

Reviews of the album were mixed. A number of critics dismissed *Some Hearts* as a bland and predictable effort. Eric R. Danton of the *Harford Courant* called it "a slick, polished collection of forgettable, country-lite ballads." But others echoed the more positive comments of music critic Bill Lamb, who called *Some Hearts* "a well-balanced blend of mainstream pop and country music. . . . Carrie Underwood sounds as comfortable in both pop and country worlds as artists like Faith Hill or Shania Twain." Reviewers such as *Houston Chronicle* critic Joey Guerrain, meanwhile, observed that Underwood's "soaring vocal range . . . takes flight when paired with the right material."

The country music community, meanwhile, embraced Underwood and *Some Hearts* with open arms. In 2006 the Academy of Country Music designated "Jesus, Take the Wheel" as its single record of the year. Academy voters also named her the best female vocalist of the year. In addition, Underwood picked up a Dove award from the Gospel Music Association and awards for best female video and best breakthrough video at the Country Music Television awards.

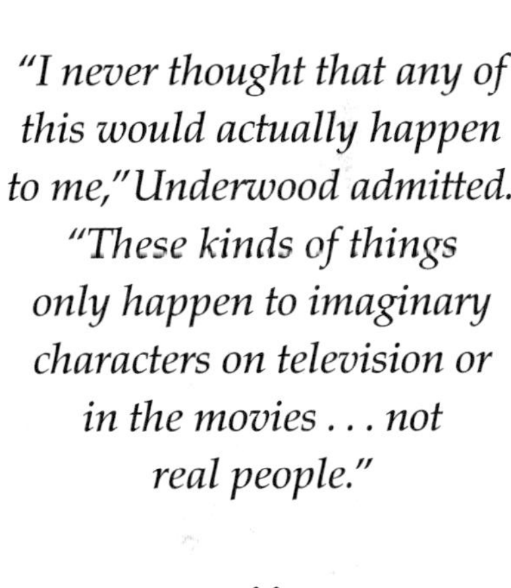

In April 2006 Underwood launched a six-month concert tour to promote *Some Hearts*. A few dates were solo, but in most instances she opened shows for established country superstars like Kenny Chesney. After watching her perform, Chesney expressed admiration for her performing style. "She connects with the audience in ways most new acts take years to develop," he declared. In early 2007, Underwood was thrilled to win three Grammy Awards, for best new artist and for best country song and best female country vocal performance, both for "Jesus, Take the Wheel."

A Cinderella Story

Underwood admits that she sometimes still can't believe that she went from being an everyday college student to a national music sensation in a matter of weeks. "I never thought that any of this would actually happen to me," she said. "These kinds of things only happen to imaginary characters on television or in the movies . . . not real people."

Underwood acknowledges that the changes to her life have sometimes been disorienting. "After I won the title of 'American Idol 2005,' a whirlwind soon followed. I was swept away to talk shows, photo shoots, and, of course, recording my very first album," she said. But she considers herself to be blessed. "I have known all of my life that being a country music singer would be the most wonderful thing that I could ever do. I am so grateful that I have this opportunity. . . . Life has changed for the better because I get to do what I love to do."

Success has not affected Underwood's close relationship with her family. In fact, she said that winning "American Idol" has made her appreciate her family more. "I miss home a lot, but I take a lot of it with me," she said. "I call home every day and talk to my sisters. I do get back as much 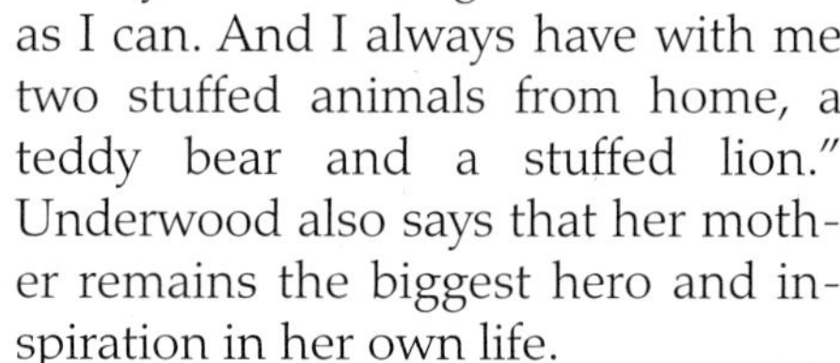
as I can. And I always have with me two stuffed animals from home, a teddy bear and a stuffed lion." Underwood also says that her mother remains the biggest hero and inspiration in her own life.

———— " ————

"I miss home a lot, but I take a lot of it with me," Underwood said. "I call home every day and talk to my sisters. I do get back as much as I can. And I always have with me two stuffed animals from home, a teddy bear and a stuffed lion."

———— " ————

As for her next career step, Underwood hopes to record more of her own songs on her next album. "I think writing is a huge gift, and some people can and some people can't, just like some people can sing and some can't sing," she said. "If I turn out to be a horrible writer then obviously I'm going to leave it up to those who do it best. But I definitely would like to try my best to have a hand in it, because then it's so much more personal."

HOME AND FAMILY

Underwood owns a two-story house in Nashville that she shares with a dog and two cats. She classifies herself as single but "never not looking." She admits that "my original plan was to get married at 24 or 25, [start having] kids around 27 and be done by 30. I don't think that's going to work out. There's too much going on."

HOBBIES AND OTHER INTERESTS

Underwood is passionate about animals and animal welfare. Although she grew up in a town where many people made their living in the cattle industry, she became a vegetarian in her teens. "My friends would raise cows. . . . Then they'd butcher and eat them," she said. "I would feel horri-

Underwood performing on "The Tonight Show with Jay Leno," October 2006.

bly guilty and couldn't do it." She has worked in the past for the Humane Society, and in 2006 she became a spokesperson for People for the Ethical Treatment of Animals.

In her spare time, Underwood loves to watch horror movies. She is a big fan of *Star Trek: The Next Generation,* Dallas Cowboys football, and chocolate. Her CD collection includes her three favorite records: *Martina*

McBride's Greatest Hits; Always & Forever, by Randy Travis; and *In Your Honor,* by Foo Fighters. It also features music by Green Day, Rascal Flatts, Garth Brooks, Loretta Lynn, and John Denver.

CREDITS

Some Hearts, 2006

SELECTED HONORS AND AWARDS

American Idol: 2005
Teen Choice Award: 2005, Choice Reality Star—Female
Best New Female Vocalist (Academy of Country Music): 2006
Single Record of the Year (Academy of Country Music): 2006, for "Jesus, Take the Wheel"
Female Vocalist of the Year (Country Music Association): 2006
Horizon Award (Country Music Association): 2006
Top New Female Vocalist (Country Music Association): 2006
Best Female Video and Breakthrough Video (Country Music Television): 2006, for "Jesus, Take the Wheel"
Dove Award (Gospel Music Association): 2006, Country Recorded Song of the Year for "Jesus, Take the Wheel"
Grammy Awards (The Recording Academy): 2007 (three awards), Best New Artist, Best Country Song, for "Jesus, Take the Wheel," and Best Female Country Vocal Performance, for "Jesus, Take the Wheel"

FURTHER READING

Books

Tracy, Kathleen. *Carrie Underwood,* 2006

Periodicals

Girls' Life, June-July 2006, p.40
Houston Chronicle, Nov. 3, 2006, "Star" section, p.1
People, June 13, 2005, p.79; Nov. 14, 2005, p.147; Nov. 6, 2006, p.38
Reader's Digest, June 2006, p.132
Self, Apr. 2006, p.64
St. Louis Post-Dispatch, Aug. 31, 2006, p.9
Teen People, June-July 2006, p.54; Sep. 2006, p.84
TV Guide, June 12, 2005, p.28; Aug. 7, 2006, p.18

ADDRESS

Carrie Underwood
Arista Records
1400 18th Avenue South
Nashville, TN 37212

WORLD WIDE WEB SITES

http://www.carrieunderwoodofficial.com
http://www.americanidol.com
http://www.americanidolmusic.com

Photo and Illustration Credits

Front cover photos: Alexander: AP Images; Ferrell: Peter Iovino, SMPSP/TM & copyright © 2004 Dreamworks LLC; Oliver: photograph copyright © David Eustace; Underwood: NBC Photo/Paul Drinkwater.

Shaun Alexander: Peter Brouillet/WireImage.com (p. 9); AP Images (front cover, pp. 11, 19); Kent Gidley/University of Alabama (p. 15); Otto Greule/Getty Images (p. 17); Kevin Terrell/WireImage.com (p. 21).

Chris Brown: Hachi/Zomba Label Group (pp. 26, 33); Scott Gries/Getty Images (p. 31); Alfeo Dixon/copyright © 2006 Screen Gems, Inc. (p. 34); CD: CHRIS BROWN (p) & copyright © 2005 Zomba Recording LLC (p. 89).

Aaron Dworkin: MacArthur Foundation (p. 38); Maciek Gregorsky (p. 41); Cibele Newman (p. 44); Jeffrey Sauger, Triest Photographic (p. 49).

Will Ferrell: Richard Foreman/TM & copyright © 2003 Dreamworks LLC (p. 53); Norman Ng/UPI/Landov (p. 58); Kerri Haynes and Marni Grossman/ copyright © 1999 Columbia Pictures Industries Inc. (p. 61, top); DVD: A NIGHT AT THE ROXBURY TM & copyright © 1998, 1999 by Paramount Pictures (p. 61, middle); Melinda Sue Gordon/TM & copyright © 2001 by Paramount Pictures (p. 61, bottom); Elliott Marks/TM & copyright © 2003 Dreamworks LLC (p. 62, top); ELF copyright © 2003 New Line Productions, Inc. Copyright © 2004 New Line Home Entertainment, Inc. (p. 62, bottom); Frank Masi, SMPSP/TM & copyright © 2004 Dreamworks LLC (p. 65); Suzanne Hanover, SMPSP/copyright © 2006 Columbia Pictures Industries, Inc. and GH One LLC (p. 67); Ralph Nelson/copyright © 2006 Columbia Pictures, Inc. (p. 68). Front cover photograph Peter Iovino, SMPSP/TM & copyright © 2004 Dreamworks LLC.

Sarah Blaffer Hrdy: John Pickering/Anthro-Photo (p. 71); Dan Hrdy/Anthro-Photo (pp. 73, 79). Book cover: MOTHER NATURE (Pantheon) copyright © Sarah Blaffer Hrdy. Jacket copyright © 1999 Random House, Inc. (p. 176).

Keira Knightley: NBC (p. 82); DVD: BEND IT LIKE BECKHAM copyright © 2002 Twentieth Century Fox Film Corporation. Copyright © 2003 TCFHE (p. 86, top); Elliott Marks, SMPSP/copyright © Disney Enterprises, Inc. and Jerry Bruckheimer, Inc. All rights reserved (p. 86, bottom); copyright © Buena Vista Home Entertainment, Inc. All rights reserved (p. 89); Alex Bailey/copyright © 2005 Focus Features LLC (p. 90); copyright © Disney. All rights reserved (p. 93).

Sofia Mulanovich: Karen Wilson/ASP/Getty Images (pp. 98, 106); Allsport AUS/Getty Images (pp. 103, 104).

Jamie Oliver: courtesy Food Network Canada (pp. 109, 117); courtesy TLC (front cover, pp. 112, 118). Book cover: THE NAKED CHEF (Hyperion) copyright © Optomen Television and Jamie Oliver, 2000. Front cover photograph copyright © David Eustace (p. 114).

Michael Sessions: Douglas Coon (pp. 123, 126, 129).

Kate Spade: Matthew Peyton/Getty Images (p. 131); LAN/Retna (p. 133); Camera Press/Circe Hamilton/Retna (p. 136); Bravo Photo/Barbara Nitke (p. 139).

Carrie Underwood: Andrew Southam/Arista Nashville (p. 143); Kevin Winter/Getty Images (p. 147); NBC Photo/Paul Drinkwater (p. 153 and front cover). CD: SOME HEARTS (Arista Nashville) (p. 150).

Cumulative Names Index

This cumulative index includes the names of all individuals profiled in *Biography Today* since the debut of the series in 1992.

 For cumulative general, places of birth, and birthday indexes, please see biographytoday.com.

For cumulative general, places of birth, and birthday indexes, please see biographytoday.com.

 For cumulative general, places of birth, and birthday indexes, please see biographytoday.com.

For cumulative general, places of birth, and birthday indexes, please see biographytoday.com.

 For cumulative general, places of birth, and birthday indexes, please see biographytoday.com.

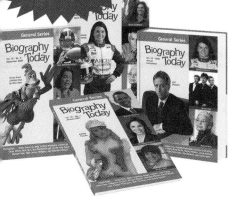